# FOLK ART IN THE ATTIC

Designed and published by Sonderho Press.
Edited by Maria Ford, Kaszas Marketing.

Printed in the United States of America.

ISBN: 978-0-9917484-4-0

This book is printed on acid-free paper.

Cover photo: The author with his special friend "Tony" (the French bulldog)
taking a break from unloading antiques, May 2014.

# Folk Art in the Attic

## Adventures from a Lifetime of Hunting for Antiques and Folk Art

Shaun Markey

Sonderho Press, Ottawa

# DEDICATION

This book is dedicated to my wife, Joan Markey, who has supported my pursuit of Canadian antiques and folk art with good humour, patience, understanding, and enthusiasm for over 30 years. And, to my son, Christopher "Teddy" Markey, who, as a boy, accompanied me on any number of trips up and down the Ottawa Valley searching for antiques when I am sure he would have preferred doing something else. I am sincerely grateful to you both.

# Table of Contents

My grandmother, Bertha Markey (nee Black), and her log house in Throoptown ON. c. 1915.

# PREFACE

A grainy black and white clipping of a photograph taken in about 1915 shows my paternal grandmother standing in front of her family's log homestead in the village of Throoptown in Eastern Ontario. The photograph at the back of a family album, reproduced in the *Prescott Journal* newspaper in the 1950s, fascinated me 30 years ago and I made a decision to find that log home. Although I didn't know it at the time, that decision would be the catalyst that propelled me into the world of Canadian antiques and folk art, a pursuit that has produced many fascinating adventures along the way, a small number of which are captured in this book.

Although the log building in the photo had been moved, I did find its original location. Wandering around the empty field where the home once stood, Joan, then my girlfriend, discovered several pottery shards, which we gathered up, placed carefully in a box, and took home. I delivered them to my mother, who has a talent for solving puzzles of any kind, and she successfully glued the fragments back together. The result of my mother's effort was a restored six-gallon butter churn with the words, *"Gallagher and McCauley, Dealers in Groceries, Crockery, Wines and Spirits, Prescott, Ont."* incised boldly on the front of the vessel.

That butter churn became a symbol to me of my family's history in Canada. I could hold it in my hands and imagine my ancestors working with it on that farm 100 years ago.

When Joan and I met that year, 1980, one of our first dates was attending a country auction in Finch, Ontario, where we witnessed an enthusiastic crowd buying many interesting antiques and collectibles. After that auction, I knew that I wanted to learn all I could about Canadian antiques and to start to acquire the objects that earlier generations of Canadians had created so carefully to use in their homes and on their farms.

Many of the things I have bought, sold, and kept in my personal

i

collection have come through "picking", the process of finding antiques by visiting farms and homes and buying items directly from the owners. But picking isn't the only method of acquiring antiques. I've purchased many items at auctions, bought items from other dealers and collectors, found great things at flea markets, and made literally hundreds of amazing finds at yard, garage, and estate sales. I've advertised for antiques in newspapers in Ottawa, Toronto, and many small towns in Eastern Ontario, often with astonishingly good results.

As any antique collector can attest, antiques can and do turn up in the most unusual places. That is part of the fun and the excitement – never knowing what you might find and where you might find it. Along with the objects, there are the many, many great characters I've met through antiques, some of whom, sadly, are now gone. Yet I continue to make new friends through antiques, friends who share the same passion as I do for discovering, restoring, and possessing examples of Canadian antiques, folk art, and other collectables.

There has been some bitterness over antiques as well. Anytime more than one person desires an object and money is involved, there is the potential for conflict. And although I have been involved in some unpleasant situations regarding antiques, happily, those experiences have been few and far between.

Throughout my many years involved with antiques, I have never relied on them as the sole source of my income. It has always been a pastime, albeit one that, from time to time, seems to dominate most everything else in life. While I haven't had to rely on antiques for my living, I know many antique dealers who do and I have profound respect for their commitment. There is nothing certain in life and perhaps nothing less certain than the business of antiques. Although art and antiques will see you through good and bad times, they may not put the bread on the table all the time or at the right time!

Mine is not a museum-type collection, either in quality or quantity. I have several interesting pieces, but likely nothing Joan and I own will find its way into a reference book on ultimate pieces of Canadian antique country furniture and folk art. There are other collectors with more knowledge than I, and others with far better collections. They are more qualified than I am to write about Canadian antiques and folk art. But I nevertheless have stories to share – stories that I think will interest other enthusiasts like myself.

Rita M. Markey with the reconstructed butter churn from the "Black Family Homestead," Ottawa, ON, 1980.

Although some of the objects described in this book are unique, this book is not so much about the quality of the antiques and folk art as it is about the adventures I have experienced in finding and acquiring these objects. While my finds may not be the best – although arguably some of them were extraordinary – they are what I searched for and what I found. I hope this book successfully captures at least some of the excitement, the fun, the risk, the frustration, the gains and, occasionally, the losses that go hand in hand with the pursuit of antiques.

Finally, if you've recently decided to start collecting, don't listen to anyone who tells you it's too expensive or that there's nothing left to collect. There are many items out there for you to find, purchase, and enjoy. Have fun. Enjoy antique collecting for the great pursuit it is. Nothing will connect you more closely to your family, your community, your province, and this great country as the process of researching, hunting for, connecting with – and hopefully acquiring – special pieces of personal history.

Shaun Markey
Ottawa, Ontario
June 2014

The Bristol Gem: an exceptional early Canadian open dish-dresser, c. 1825 (Acquired 1982)

# THE BRISTOL GEM

On a lazy Easter Monday in 1982, I was kicking around the house in Ottawa doing not much of anything. Typically on a weekend, I would have been at an auction in the Ottawa Valley looking for country furniture items. However, on this particular long weekend, I was taking time off from the antique search and was determined to stay at home and do something constructive in another sense.

Then the phone rang and on the other end of the line was an old friend.

"Shaun, we were wondering what to do today and thought about going to an auction with you. How about it? Can you take us to one?"

Ken and Kate were not avid collectors so I was surprised at their request. But their call was all it took to melt my resolve about staying home that day.

"Sure", I said, without missing a beat. "I think we can do that. Let me check the papers and see what's going on." My wife, Joan, gave me a long look but true to her kind nature quickly agreed that the four of us should go.

It didn't take me long to find a farm auction near the little community of Bristol in West Quebec – about an hour's drive from Ottawa via Highway 148 on the north side of the Ottawa River.

Lieutenant Colonel John By founded Ottawa, originally called Bytown, in 1826. The city sits at the confluence of three significant rivers: the mighty Ottawa that flows southeast from Lake Timiskaming, The Gatineau, which flows south, and the Rideau, which flows north from the Upper Rideau Lake. For much of its length, the Ottawa River defines the boundary between the provinces of Ontario and Quebec. From the 1800's to 1910, the lumber barons reigned supreme. They floated squared timber on the Ottawa River east to Ottawa and then on to Montreal for shipment overseas. Once the land was cleared of forest, settlers moved in to take up and farm the good "bottom" land near the river.

I remember being a child and the drive up to our cottage about an hour north of Ottawa. The road followed the Gatineau River and for miles the entire surface of the river would be filled, shore to shore, and as far north as you could see, with short pulp logs being floated down to the mills at Hull, Buckingham, and Masson, Quebec. It was a river of wood.

One contemporary company out of Norway Bay, a community on the Ottawa, has made a viable business of rescuing the white pine logs that long ago sank to the bottom of the Ottawa River and its tributaries. Despite being submerged for over 100 years, the logs are, once dried, still quite useable and in demand for various applications.

I called Ken and Kate back and the four of us agreed to take in this particular auction. Off we went. The village of Bristol is situated opposite an area of the Ottawa River called Lac des Chats, directly across from the Town of Arnprior, Ontario.

While auctions can be productive, they have risks. Even for experienced collectors and dealers, they can be emotionally intense experiences. My preference is to buy privately, and although I know of one or two collectors who have never attended an auction or refuse to buy at them, the majority of collectors and dealers routinely do buy at public auctions.

When I read the listing for the Bristol auction in the newspaper, nothing in particular caught my eye. It was a general farm sale with all the usual items one would expect to find at a sale of this type. Of course there were antiques, but that's not surprising. Most sales at that time included antiques. Farms offer lots of storage space that generation after generation of a family would use. Unwanted furniture and other items were routinely trundled off into barn lofts, equipment sheds, and attics, where they would remain for years. Often, a case piece of furniture would be repurposed and put to use storing tools, paint cans, preserves, or any number of other items. For the most part, as long as furniture is kept reasonably dry and protected, it will last indefinitely.

As I think back to the decades of the 1980s and into the 1990s, despite the complaints of experienced dealers and pickers about the lack of quality and quantity, those were my halcyon collecting days. There were usually several farm auctions each weekend and most of them offered up good early antique items of interest. Of course, my knowledge and experience were limited at the time, so I didn't buy much at first. But I saw what others were buying and I learned from observation and discussion.

Knowledge doesn't come quickly or easily, and as much as I wanted to reach a higher level of understanding, it was not going to happen overnight.

I could only envy the pickers and dealers I knew in Eastern Ontario, some of whom had already been in the business for 15 to 20 years. One individual in particular had picked literally hundreds of great cupboards.

Like most novice collectors, in the beginning I stripped and refinished most of the antique furniture I found. After two years, I made a transition and by 1983 was determined to build a collection of only items with original finish or acceptable over paint. Of course, establishing an objective is one thing; realizing it is an entirely different matter. As I said, though, conditions at that time were enabling. There was a lot of material coming out at farm auctions, pickers were routinely finding great things in the Ottawa Valley, and even yard sales produced surprisingly good finds. It was not uncommon, for example, to find decorated merchant stoneware at yard sales. I have at least three very nice examples today in my collection, all found at yard sales. Even good cupboards and harvest tables could be found at yard sales back then.

While I attended auctions, it wasn't long before I decided to try my own hand at "picking" – going door-to-door, farm-to-farm, enquiring about antiques for sale. I wanted to buy objects direct from a barn or an attic. I wanted to know without a shadow of a doubt exactly from where an item had come. It's true, too, that objects bought directly from the owner can be had for less money (although on occasion I have discovered, to my chagrin, that's not always the case). Finally, I wanted the "thrill" – that emotional rush that happens when you discover something great that has been hidden or neglected for years. As a collector, once you've had that feeling, you want it again and again.

Back then there were few if any television shows about antiques; only the occasional article in the newspaper; and there certainly was no Internet, the medium that transformed antique collecting and dealing, for better or for worse, in the late 1990s. There were, however, excellent reference books. The veritable bibles on Canadian antiques by Philip Shackleton (*The Furniture of Old Ontario*) and Howard Pain (*The Heritage of Upper Canadian Furniture*) had been published and there were several others to which one could refer.

Typically, though, in the antiques field one was self-taught. You learned lessons the hard way, which usually involved losing money. Nothing teaches you more about antiques than when you are financially invested in a piece, especially if you ultimately lose some or all of that investment.

After arriving at the Bristol auction and parking the car in an adjacent field, we made our way to the sale, signed for a registration number and

Kate and Ken Lindsay, with Joan Markey, aboard the Quyon Ferry on the way to the auction in Bristol, QC, May 1982.

started looking at the various items on offer. The crowd of 100-or-so people was focused on the auctioneer selling items from the top of a large wagon. Not being interested in what was being sold at the moment, I walked on my own past the crowd. I had taken a few steps across the open area of the yard when I stopped in my tracks. There, leaning up against a lamp pole to the right of the doorway of an equipment shed, was an antique pine cupboard. Not just any pine cupboard. This was an open dish-dresser, a rare and early form of antique country furniture.

I walked directly to it. As I stood in front of the piece, the boxes on my mental checklist for cupboards immediately filled with check marks. First of all, it was pine, one of the most desirable species of wood, and while the surface wasn't original, it was a very old, dry, grey over paint and perfectly acceptable.

Remarkably, the piece originally had "shoe feet" – narrow lengths of wood at the bottom of each side that supported the cupboard and kept the case slightly elevated off the floor. One of the rounded ends that extended out from the front edge of the cupboard and looked like a little boot or foot was missing, but I knew it could be restored. Across the front of the cupboard at the bottom edge, running the width of the piece between the shoe feet, was a generous and wavy cutout – a detail that was decidedly better than merely a straight board or plinth-type base moulding.

Yet another attractive feature was the fact that the sides of the base didn't simply end under the edges of the open counter at its waist, but continued upward past the counter to end in decorative semi circles. While not as detailed as the lower section, the upper part of the cupboard was finished nicely with a generous crown moulding. The open shelves were nicely intact. The cupboard back showed wide pit-sawn boards and hand-forged nails, further evidence of an early date of construction.

The front of the flat paneled doors showed signs of once having *H/L* hinges, likely hand-forged. And while they had been replaced, it did not detract from the piece.

In short, I was looking at a very early, exceptional Canadian cupboard, quite possibly as early as 1825 and perhaps even earlier.

I rushed over to Joan. "There is an amazing cupboard over there and I want to stay here to bid on it." Fortunately, Joan and our friends agreed. They too, wanted to share in the excitement of battling for this excellent Canadian cupboard. We settled in for the wait until the cupboard came under the hammer. A couple of hours later, the auctioneer and the crowd finally turned their attention to the open dish-dresser. I stood a few rows back in the crowd.

My only recollection now is that I got in on the bidding fairly early and stayed in. There was only one other serious bidder and the bids went up in small increments until the auctioneer looked at me for a bid of $800 – a lot of money in 1982. I didn't hesitate and nodded in the affirmative. The auctioneer turned to my opponent looking for an increase on my bid. It never came. After another pause, Revel Stewart, the auctioneer, knocked the cupboard down to me for $800. What a great feeling! The cupboard was mine. I couldn't help thinking that if it weren't for my friend's phone call, I wouldn't even have bothered going to the auction. Now, as fate had it, I had found an extraordinary piece of Canadiana and successfully purchased it. Later that day, the dish-dresser was housed safely in my garage in Ottawa.

A few days later, I started to fret about the money I had spent on the cupboard. The $800 had come from savings Joan and I had set aside for a down payment on a new house. During the week, it continued to bother me until I finally put a call into a dealer friend of mine and told him about the piece and that I wanted to sell it. We made arrangements for him and his wife to drop by our apartment that evening. We spent an hour or two chatting until he finally made a move to leave. I walked him and his wife down to their truck. Just as his hand was on the handle of the door he said:

"What about that cupboard Shaun?"

"Well, it's in the garage. Come and have a look at it."

We walked down the laneway to the garage. It was dusk but there was still plenty of visibility. I swung open the garage door and stood back to give him a clear view of the cupboard. He was quiet and didn't say a word for a minute or so while he took in the cupboard. Then, with his best poker face he turned to me.

"What did you want for it?"

I paused. I hated to see the cupboard go but something inside of me was forcing me to sell. "$1,100 dollars", I said quietly.

Without another word, he reached into his pocket and counted out the money. A moment later, he backed up his truck to the door and we loaded the cupboard into it.

After a few months, the memory of that cupboard faded. I missed it, but life was busy. We bought the new house and moved in. My job in government kept me well occupied during the week. Come the weekends, Joan and I would look for auctions to attend, hoping to find inexpensive but quality Canadian country furniture to add to our small but slowly expanding collection.

I continued to sell things to the dealer who bought the open dish-dresser and also bought a few items from him, including a terrific c. 1870 pine sideboard in original colour from Perth, Ontario that is still in my collection.

Antique dealers are notorious for playing their cards close to their chest for fear of letting slip a detail that will enable a competitor to gain an advantage. Although I asked on more than one occasion, he avoided telling me what had happened to the cupboard. He acknowledged selling it to a dealer in the U.S., a common occurrence in those days, but would never identify the individual or the store. At times I thought about trying to find the cupboard and repurchase it for our collection. I told him that was my motivation but the information was never forthcoming.

That following winter, Joan and I were on a day trip in upstate New York, not far from the Canada / U.S. border. As part of our trip, we dropped into a few antique stores. We were in the last one of the day and headed toward the exit when Joan exclaimed.

"Shaun! There's your open dish-dresser."

She was right. There against a wall was the Bristol gem. I stared at it in disbelief. My next thought was to buy it back. I turned casually to the owner.

"By the way, how much is that cupboard there by the door?"

"Oh," she said. "That cupboard will never be for sale. It's one of our absolute favourites and a very early and a rare form."

"I know", I said. "I used to own that cupboard."

And with that we said our good-byes and headed back, somewhat forlornly, to home.

Since that Easter Monday in 1982, I've found and purchased several more open dish-dressers, two of which I still own. Today, it is rare to find a good cupboard when picking or at auction. But every now and then, a good example emerges. And, that's what keeps us all going: the thought that just around the next turn in the road, just inside the next shed or in a back room, we'll find an undiscovered cupboard. To this day, I still think about the one that I let get away – the Bristol gem from the auction I almost missed.

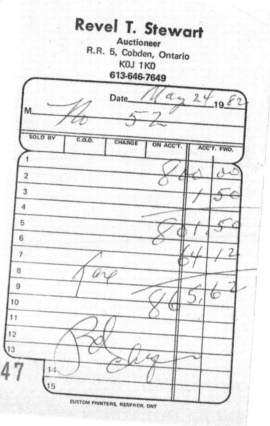

Folk art items from the "Attic" purchase, 1984.

# 2

## FOLK ART IN THE ATTIC

E arly on in my collecting life, I developed a fascination with folk art. This was about 30 years ago, and at the time most of the attention was being paid to traditional or historical folk art. But I was inclined toward contemporary folk art, which was just as much fun to collect, easier to find, and more affordable.

In those early days I'd had some luck finding folk art in and around the Ottawa Valley, including the work of Arthur Sauvé (1896-1973), an amazing wood carver with a genius for interpreting his artistic visions and realizing them in wood. Although he carved wildlife, shelves, picture frames, religious items, and storage cases for musical instruments, Sauvé also experimented with mechanical elements in his carvings, as evidenced by his articulated "man on a bike" whirligigs, of which only three are known to exist. Two are in Canadian museums and the other, which I found and owned for a time, is now in a private collection.

In the Upper Ottawa Valley the wildlife-themed carvings of Abe Patterson (1899-1969) are well known and highly sought after to this day. There is also the work of Charles Vollrath (1870-1952) from Chalk River, Ontario. While he also carved animals, sometimes of impressive size and scale, Mr. Vollrath also produced carvings in a smaller format. His winged angels are a prime example, executed in a naive, almost spiritual, yet highly skilled manner. I would put these artists on a par with the famous Bourgault brothers of Saint-Jean-Port-Joli, Quebec, although the carvings produced by these men are so elegant and well executed that they might be viewed more as fine art than folk art. Regardless, their work, in my opinion, is among the most inspired and magnificent art ever produced in Canada.

Art Dixon (1917-2011) was a carver I met in Pembroke in 1983. A quiet, gentle man, Dixon's basement was filled with wonderful woodcarvings of all shapes and sizes. His three-and four-foot high examples of lumberjacks, bears, and other characters always produce a smile on the face of anyone who sees them. He also painted his carvings with bright and varied colours that added to their appeal. Like most folk artists, Dixon was surprised when I expressed interest in buying his carvings but he was happy to oblige. His carving of a lumberjack playing an accordion, mouth wide singing a song, complete with hearts tattooed on his upper arms, remains one of the favourite pieces in my collection. I sold the original but Dixon was kind enough to sell me another version at a later date.

I once came across an elderly man in Brockville who, during our roadside conversation, told me he painted pictures and then invited me into his home to see his work. As we stepped into the front hallway, I wasn't prepared for what came next. The hallway extended the length of the house toward a rear kitchen. On my right was the entrance to the living room with its dining room. It seemed that every square inch of the walls in the hallway and the adjoining rooms was covered with his paintings. He had hung his artwork from floor to ceiling. We wandered slowly through his collection.

I liked several pieces and when it seemed like an appropriate time I asked about purchasing one work in particular. It was a memory painting. The image was of a young girl skipping rope in the summer kitchen of an old farmhouse. All of the items were clearly depicted in the painting, including a cast iron stove, harvest table, and other pieces of furniture. He looked somewhat startled at my request to buy one.

"All the time I've painted. All these years, I've never sold a painting. You're the first person who's ever asked to buy one", he said quietly.

"No!" I replied, taken aback by his statement. "Not one single person has even asked to buy a painting?"

"Very few people have even seen them," he replied.

"Well, I think your paintings are terrific. And I'd like to buy one today."

By that time we had returned to the front hallway and I pointed to the large painting of the young girl skipping rope.

"That one there. I really like it. I'll give you $75 for it."

He gazed at the painting and turned to me.

"Really. You'd buy that painting from me for $75?"

"Definitely," I said. "Right now."

He returned his gaze to the painting and stared at it again for some time. He turned to me.

"No, I can't sell it," he said. "I just can't."

"Seagull" by Joe Norris, 1981.

Although disappointed, I wasn't surprised by his response. He had spent years painting those pictures. They decorated his home and he lived with them. While art is bought and sold routinely everywhere in the world, to this man the concept of selling one of his paintings was totally foreign. And while he was perhaps tempted by the thought and quietly flattered that I asked him, he could not bring himself to sell even one of his works. I took "no" for an answer and we said goodbye.

As the years went by, I often thought about him and occasionally drove by his house when I was passing through Brockville. Then one day a few years after I had first met him, I drove by and the house had a For Sale sign on the front lawn. I stopped and asked next door what had happened. As his neighbour stood at the front door, I couldn't help notice that behind her on the walls of her home were several of the paintings done by the man next door. I got the impression from her that when he left, his family emptied the contents of his home including his paintings. There was little if any family interest in them and they invited her to take them so she gathered up a number of them to use in her home. Like him, ironically, she didn't want to

"Cat" by Joe Sleep, 1985.

sell any of them. So, try as I might, I was apparently never going to own one of this man's paintings, and that remains true to this day.

Eastern Ontario and the Ottawa Valley has its share of brilliant folk artists and I enjoyed collecting their works, but it wasn't long before I was also drawn to the joyful paintings of Maud Lewis and the impressive work of Joe Norris and other folk artists from Atlantic Canada.

One summer, about 1987, Joan and I decided to drive to Nova Scotia and look for the work of Maud Lewis, a well-known folk artist. Not surprisingly, we did find some, but the prices, about $1,500 each, were too daunting for us. (Little did we know the prices for Lewis paintings would often exceed $10,000 and more, 20 years later). We satisfied ourselves buying other art and antiques that were fun and exciting to find.

At a motel one evening during the trip, a Quebec picker pulled in with his truck piled high with things. I bought a very nice Flack and Van Arsdale crock from him and we had a good chat.

This was the first of two trips we made out east. The second also yielded no Maud Lewis paintings but lots of other interesting folk art and antique finds.

Later that same year, one very cold winter evening, I was in the kitchen at home in Ottawa when the phone rang and the chap on the other end of the line asked, "Is this Shaun Markey?"

"Yes it is," I replied.

"My mother gave me your business card and it says you buy folk art?"

"Yes, I buy folk art," was my reply. "Do you have a piece you want to sell?"

I can remember thinking at the time, who is this guy and what could he possibly have that would interest me?

"Well," he said, "actually I have several pieces that I want to sell. It's a collection I put together when I lived out east."

"What artists do you have in the collection?" I asked, rather abruptly, because I was certain he would describe artists in whom I had little interest.

"Oh," he said, "there is a Maud Lewis, two paintings by Joe Norris, some by Joe Sleep, carvings by Charlie Tanner and a bunch of other stuff."

Lewis, Norris, Sleep, Tanner! My goodness, I thought, these are exactly the artists I want to collect and I've driven twice to Nova Scotia and come back without anything by any of them.

"Where are you?" I said, trying to keep the excitement out of my voice.

He named a street in Ottawa that was literally one minute from my house. I could have crawled there on my hands and knees in 20 minutes and would have gladly done so to have a look at this stash.

I asked when I could come and see the items.

"How about now?" he said.

"I'll be right there."

Soon, I was ringing the doorbell of a stately old home, which turned out to be his mothers' residence. After greeting me at the door, he led me to the stairs.

"The things are up in the attic. I keep them stored there."

Up we went, two or three flights of stairs, until we came to the door of the attic.

As he opened it, he turned to me and said: "You'll have to excuse the temperature in here. We don't keep it heated at all." With that, he swung open the door.

In antique collecting, as in other walks of life, there are moments that stand out. With antiques, they are those spine-tingling moments when, after a great deal of searching, one comes across a significant find. Of course, locating an object you desire is only half the battle. Acquiring the object is the other half and until that happens you must balance the feeling of excitement with the tension of not knowing whether you can actually complete the acquisition. Anyone who has pursued antiques knows only too well the horrible feeling that comes with losing an item to someone else or, for some other reason, not being able to buy it.

The first glimpse of the contents of that room was memorable. It was an unfinished attic with a sharply sloped ceiling that angled toward the floor. All around the edges of the room, propped up against the walls, was a row of paintings, sculptures, and carvings by some terrific Canadian folk artists, including Maud Lewis, Joe Norris, Joe Sleep, Charlie Tanner, Collins Eisenhauer, and others, plus several more unsigned but impressive folk art examples – about thirty pieces in all.

Included in the group was a beautiful scene of a cart and driver by Maud Lewis. There was a superb "cove scene" by Joe Norris with his characteristic pink sky in a frame decorated with birds, and another Joe Norris "seagull portrait". I noticed one of Charlie Tanner's neat "duck boat" carvings, which featured a hunter with a dozen miniature decoys on its deck and several more tethered to it, meant to float adjacent to the boat as they would in the water in real life.

I stood there in the middle of a freezing room, teeth chattering and shivering from the cold and probably the excitement, too.

I thought to myself, "There's too much. I can't handle this or afford it. What am I going to do?" I wandered slowly about the room, picking up one piece after the other. I kept up some meaningless banter while I tried to figure out a plan. Perhaps, I thought, I can buy one or two of the best things, like the Maud Lewis and the Joe Norris, and leave it at that. I broached the subject of a partial purchase but he knew wisely that to sell one or two of the best items would seriously undermine the value of the remaining collection.

"No," he said, when I asked. "I want to sell the whole collection at once. I don't want to break it up. It's been in storage for years because we moved around and it's time for it to go."

After a final look around the room, we left and went back downstairs to the front hall. We stood there for what seemed like an eternity. I knew it was now or never. I could not leave empty handed.

I don't remember the actual words we exchanged at that moment. However, he quoted me a price of around $2,000, which was a lot of money to me at the time. I agreed to the price, or a figure close to it, and wrote the cheque there and then. The next hour or so was spent making trips back and forth to the attic to retrieve the works of art and put them carefully into my vehicle.

I drove the short distance home. How many times does a wife hear the words: "Honey, I just bought a folk art collection!" It was a first for my house, that's for sure. True to form, Joan was entirely supportive of the pur-

A cove scene by Joe Norris, 1981.

chase and she enjoyed the moment as I brought the pieces in to show her.

At the time, I was part of an antique market in the south end of Ottawa. I decided to mount a show and sale of maritime folk art featuring all of the collection. To this day, it remains, however modest in scale, the only show and sale of purely Canadian folk art to be staged in Ottawa. The event ran for a week and sales were reasonably good, despite the recession we were mired in at that time. There were some follow-on sales after the fact, as well. What didn't sell found its way back into my collection.

Since that day, I've continued to search for and find several more examples of work by these artists. Whenever I see their work, be it by Lewis, Norris, Tanner, or any of the other artists in that collection, it brings back the memory of that winter evening when a simple phone call led me to one of the most memorable purchases in my collecting career.

L. Gilmour and Jack Darragh playing cards from set C55, 1911.

# A Shoebox in Martintown

I n the course of 30 years of collecting, I have dragged my siblings, often reluctantly, into various and sundry escapades involving antiques. An auction in 1984 attended by my brother, Scott and I, is one example.

I've forgotten now what prompted me to go to the auction or to ask Scott to accompany me, but that Saturday morning found us in the village of Martintown in Eastern Ontario. The villages in Glengarry County are some of the first and oldest settlements in that part of the province. On this particular day, a crowd had gathered behind a modest but quite old frame house on the main street, in anticipation of buying the antique furniture and collectables arranged outside on the back porch and around the perimeter of the rear yard.

These were the early days of my collecting career and I had barely developed an eye for anything, let alone for country furniture in original paint, which would become my primary interest a few years later. I recall now that there was a very nice glazed flat-to-the wall cupboard in a faux mahogany finish; the effect is achieved with the use of a dark red paint first layer with black painted feather graining over top of that. I wasn't in the league of collectors who bought cupboards then, although I certainly wanted to be.

Looking around the various items to be auctioned, a couple of things did rouse our interest. The first was a shoebox full of old cards that came as promotional items in cigarette packages. There were all different types, including sports themes like hockey and lacrosse, a series devoted to exotic animal species, and more. For some reason, I decided to bid on them. Scott was on board with the plan. I thought $100 ought to do it.

The other item was an antique reference book: *The Encyclopedia of the Gasoline Engine*. A boat restorer friend of mine had asked me to keep my eye open for a book called *Diseases of the Gasoline Engine*. Although not the

P. Moran and R. Power playing cards from set C55, 1911.

exact title, I thought he'd want to have this one.

The auction got underway a short time later and we sat down on a couple of wooden chairs about half way back in the crowd. Item after item came under the hammer and the contents of the home were sold one by one to the highest bidders. An hour or two into the auction, the shoebox of cards came up for sale.

The bidding opened at $25. In a matter of seconds we had reached my $100 limit and, disgusted, I shook my head "no" when the auctioneer looked to me for another bid. I breathed a sigh of frustration and sat back in my chair.

What happened next took me completely by surprise. Scott suddenly put up his hand, signaling another bid to the auctioneer.

"Scotty! What are you doing?!" I hissed.

There was no response. He didn't even turn to look at me. Eyes forward, he just kept responding to the auctioneer, putting his hand up to advance the bid when it was his turn to do so.

$110, $130, $150!" the auctioneer called out the bids.

"Scotty! It's too much…!" I whispered fiercely.

He never faltered. I was speechless.

"$170, $180, $190, $200, $210!" the auctioneer yelled out while pointing back and forth to Scotty and the competing bidder.

On they went, two determined bidders. Scott wasn't backing down.

"$220…$230, $240, $250…!" The crowd was absolutely silent, mesmerized by the contest playing out before them.

At the $250 dollar figure the other bidder had had enough. The auctioneer paused, looked around.

"Any other advance on $250? I am going to sell it at $250! Sold!" Scott was victorious and held his card up so they could record his bidder number.

"Jesus H. Christ!" I said. "You bought them!"

Scott turned to me: "Yes. I wanted them."

I just shook my head and laughed. I had discovered that when my brother wants something, he is one determined individual.

The shoebox full of cards arrived at our chairs, passed down through the audience until it came to us. We briefly looked at the contents before Scott put the lid back in place and held the box safely on his lap. The auction continued and it was about an hour later when the auctioneer stopped the proceedings and reached into the box lot immediately in front of him that was next to be sold. As we watched, he extracted one single card.

"Who bought that lot of cards in the shoebox a while back?" he asked.

Scott put up his hand.

"Here," the auctioneer said. "This belongs to you. Pass it back to him."

With that he passed the little card to someone in the first row who dutifully turned and gave it to someone immediately behind their seat. One by one, each recipient passed the card to the row behind until finally it arrived and Scott put his hand out and took the card. He held the card gently out in front of us by the edge with his thumb and forefinger.

We both stared at it.

It was the image of a young baseball player in a grey coloured uniform. His name was printed in small modest letters beneath the photo. The words were:

"*Ty Cobb*"

We both looked at each other incredulously.

"I think I'll put this in the box," Scott said.

"Do that." I said and we both smiled.

The auctioneer finished with the small items and moved on to other groups of things in the yard, including the book I had spotted earlier. Soon the *Encyclopedia of the Gasoline Engine* was mine for $30.

We watched as the furniture was sold, including the beautiful flat-to-the-wall cupboard in original paint. I think it brought $600, a bargain by any standard, even in 1984 dollars.

The auction ended and we made our way to the car, where we sat and examined the contents of the shoebox more closely. One group of the sporting cards caught our eye.

"Look at these Scotty," I said. "These are early hockey cards. And there's a lot of them." The cards were small, measuring only two inches in height and perhaps an inch in width. A colour-tinted image of the player was on the face of each card and a short bio was printed on the back. There were some iconic names and images on the cards, including: *Frank Patrick, Art Ross, Lester Patrick, Newsy Lalonde, Georges Vezina* and others. One set was complete. One set, as I recall, was missing one player. All the cards were in mint condition.

I knew when I got back to Ottawa I would have to do some research to find out more information about the cards Scott purchased that day. Of course, this was long before the Internet and research then was done the old fashioned way – by digging into reference books. Little did I know then just how early and special these cards were.

A few weeks after the sale, I came across a book with the rather mundane title of *Hockey Card Checklist and Price Guide*. When I got the book home, I opened it to see if I could find any reference to the hockey cards in the shoebox. It didn't take long. There on page seven were two sets of cards identical to the ones in the shoebox. To my astonishment, I saw that they were the first two sets listed in the book.

What Scott had bought that day were known, according to the book, as "C56" and "C55," the first two sets of hockey cards ever produced in Canada and dating to 1910 and 1911 respectively. I picked up the phone and gave Scott a call.

"You're not going to believe this," I said, and promptly told him about the reference in the book.

Of course we were both elated. Over the next few months, with the exception of the C56 and C55 sets, we slowly sold off the other cards that came from the box. If I remember correctly, Scott sold the Ty Cobb card one morning at a local flea market we attended. I think the sum realized

At an auction in the Ottawa Valley, 1984 – I'm the one in the green polo shirt.

was around $90. I am sure the collector was glad he went to the flea market that morning!

A year or two later we eventually sold C56 and C55 to a nostalgia dealer from the Ottawa area. It was a very good profit at the time, but in retrospect I wish we had kept at least one set and put the cards in a safe place. Today, even one set of those cards is worth many thousands of dollars.

That day in Martintown, I was merely a bystander. I watched my determined younger brother successfully purchase one of the all-time great auction finds in Eastern Ontario of the last 30 years…in a shoebox.

The "Lieutenant Colonel By" cupboard, as restored. c. 1840 (Acquired 1992)

# 4

# A Cupboard Fit for a Lieutenant Colonel

As it flows north toward the City of Ottawa, the Rideau River traces a route through several historic Eastern Ontario towns and villages, including Smiths Falls, Merrickville, Burritt's Rapids, Kars, and Manotick. After the war of 1812, the Rideau River became the geographic focus for the Rideau Canal Waterway, a mammoth engineering project of stone lock stations and fortifications engineered by Lieutenant Colonel John By and completed in 1832. The entire Canal is 202 kms in length and includes 45 sets of locks.

When it finally opened to traffic, the Canal made the Rideau River system navigable between Ottawa and the City of Kingston. It gave what was at the time called Upper Canada an alternate and serviceable military transport route between Montreal and Kingston other than the St. Lawrence River.

The Rideau River corridor breathes history and the farms and settlements along its shores have long been a source for exceptional Canadian country antiques. The area is dotted with solidly built, early stone homes constructed in the Georgian manner by the stonemasons who worked for Lieutenant Colonel By's canal crew. Many of those workers were granted land adjacent to the river and settled along its banks after the canal was completed.

On an early summer day in 1992, I was exploring the countryside inland from the Rideau River just south of Ottawa, hoping to find something of antique interest.

Unlike some in the business, I am not an "obsessive" picker, stopping at every single place along a concession road and buying anything and everything that has some age. At the time, I thought of myself (and still do) as a strategic picker – someone who analyzes where he might find antique country furniture, searches for places that are often overlooked for various reasons, and selectively stops at those sites.

On this particular day, I had noticed a Georgian-style limestone house on a promontory of land overlooking the paved secondary road on which I was driving. While it was a rural setting it was only a few miles south of Ottawa proper with several modern houses and a golf course nearby. Given its location, I doubted that any picker had been to this place recently.

I drove up a long gravel laneway and pulled in behind the house to a generous parking area in front of an ageing set of barn buildings. I parked my truck, and knocked on the frame of the old screen door. A moment later, the large figure of a man in his 70s appeared behind the screen, the sun partially obscuring him from view.

"Yeah, what can I do for you," he said gruffly.

"I stopped at your place because I'm looking for antiques – old pine cupboards, long tables, that type of thing. I thought you might have something like that."

"What do want 'em for?" he asked sharply.

"I buy, collect them, and restore them."

A long, uncomfortable pause followed as he considered my question.

"Well," he said slowly, almost reluctantly, "We've got one of those old cupboards in the basement."

"Would you show it to me?" I asked.

Another long, uncomfortable pause ensued as he surveyed me up and down from his position behind the screen door. "Yeah, I guess I could show it to you." With that, he pushed the screen door and held it open, granting me entrance into his home.

I love walking into a period Canadian home, even an unrestored one. The sense of time and history engulfs you. In this case, the house was over 150 years old and I noticed that the interior appointments and details were intact, albeit partially hidden by the clutter of everyday life. I glanced around as we approached a door off the kitchen.

"Let me get the light on," he said over his shoulder as he opened the door and we followed a narrow set of steps down to the cellar.

"It's over here," he said, as we turned left at the bottom of the stairs and took a few steps toward the centre of the room. There, sitting at an odd angle, part of it on the cement floor and part of it on an adjacent dirt floor, sat a canted-top, open dish-dresser. Whoever had moved the cupboard got it only so far because its cornice jammed against one of the overhead floor joists and they had left it there. It had obviously stood in that very spot for many years because the damp cellar and the dirt floor had taken a heavy toll. The cupboard's base and left side both showed significant damage from rot. More alarming was the fact the left door and the narrow section of wood to which it hinged was completely missing.

Although it had suffered from years of neglect, I could see that this was a rare and interesting cupboard and that the damaged areas were contained to the bottom and could be restored by my cabinet-maker. The missing door could also be duplicated and coloured to match the other side. The extent of the restoration meant that this cupboard would likely never be of interest to a serious collector or dealer, but I like seeing neglected pieces of country furniture restored.

"Yes," I said. "That's the type of thing I am searching for. Have you ever thought about selling it?"

"Well," said the owner, "How much would you give for it?"

The price of an antique is always a delicate subject, especially when you're buying privately. An old picker friend of mine warned me that, although they'll insist otherwise, people always have a price in mind for an object they own. The trick is to get them to divulge the figure they have in mind and not to give them your price first. After all, the two figures could be wildly different.

I stood there looking at the open dish dresser, which I knew would need a lot of restorative work. I threw caution and strategy to the winds.

"I'll give you $75 for it," I said.

"No damn way I'd sell that for $75 dollars," he retorted in disgust.

Gosh, I thought to myself, I've totally insulted him with that price and he's going to come back at me with a big figure I won't want to pay.

"Well then," I said quickly, "How much would you sell it for?"

He stood across from me, took a long glance downward, then looked up slowly.

"I wouldn't sell that cupboard for less than $100 dollars," he said defiantly.

Relieved to hear the figure, I responded, "All right, I'll give you the $100."

He pondered the offer.

"Fine then, you can have it."

I pulled a hundred dollars out of my pocket and handed it over to him.

"There's only one problem," he observed, pocketing my money. "We've changed the staircase a while back and there's no way that cupboard will fit up there anymore."

"So, how about that other entrance?" I said, pointing to a short set of stairs leading up to a set of exterior bulkhead doors that offered another way out of the basement.

"Maybe," he said. "But you might not get it up there either."

I turned my attention back to the cupboard. Due to the rot and deterioration, the left side of the piece was literally hanging on by a few hand-forged nails. I thought that if I could pull the cupboard apart into sections, the stairs wouldn't be an issue.

"Give me a minute," I said. "I've got an idea."

There was a flat automotive leaf spring propped up against the wall. I retrieved it and, using it like a lever, I wedged the iron between the left side of the cupboard and the counter portion. With a bit of coaxing the left side came away in one large piece. I did the same with some of the backboards until the cupboard was essentially reduced to its component pieces. It was then just a matter of walking the pieces up the steps, outside, and putting them in the back of my truck.

Outside, I stood back brushing the dirt and dust from my hands and clothes. The farmer stood outside the door watching me finish the task.

I couldn't stop thinking about the missing door. I knew from experience that sometimes missing parts of a piece of furniture can be found being used for some other purpose. You have to be sure to look around carefully before leaving the barn, or in this case, the basement. I turned to the farmer.

"By the way, whatever happened to the left door from that cupboard?"

"I dunno," he said. "It's been missing as long as I can remember."

"Would you mind if I went back down there and had a look around for it?

"No," he replied. "Go ahead."

With his approval, I quickly went back down the exterior staircase into the basement. That cupboard door, I thought, must be here somewhere. I knew I had only a few minutes before his patience ran out and he asked me to leave. The light was poor but I scanned the rest of the basement from the bottom of the stairs. Nothing. Then I stared across to the far corner where an old washing machine stood. To its right was a galvanized steel laundry tub sitting on two upturned plastic dairy cases. I continued looking past them. Wait! I looked again at the laundry tub. I could just make out the edge of a single board under the tub spanning the dairy cases and serving as a shelf. From my vantage point, it looked to be the right size. I quickly marched over and removed the laundry tubs covering the board. Fantastic! It was the missing door for the cupboard! And, better yet, it still had the original hand-forged hinges and attached trim section, which could easily be remounted to the left side of the cupboard. Picking up the door, I zipped back to the stairs and outside into the sunshine.

"Found it!" I exclaimed.

"So you did," the farmer said. "No extra charge for that," he added dryly.

On my way back into town, I dropped off the cupboard, in pieces, to the individual who did restoration work for me. He was excited to see the project ahead of him and assured me that he would have it ready in a week. True to his word, I soon received a call from him to pick up the cupboard. It was a pleasant surprise to see what had been essentially a pile of boards in the back of my truck fully restored. Later, I had the paint colour matched perfectly and the job was complete.

Some years after that experience, I was standing in the checkout line at the local building supply store. A voice across from me said. "Do you remember me?"

I looked up into the eyes of a tall, elderly man who was in the line up opposite me. I hesitated. I didn't recognize him. But he obviously knew me. I searched my memory. Nothing.

He smiled faintly. "You bought a cupboard from me south of here opposite the river."

Then I knew him! It was the farmer who owned the "Lieutenant Colonel By" open dish-dresser.

"Yes, I said, "Of course, now I remember."

"How did it turn out?"

"It turned out well. Really well."

"That's good. Glad to hear it."

And with that, he turned and walked away.

I own the "Lieutenant Colonel By" cupboard to this day. It is a memorable souvenir of that occasion so many years ago when my instincts paid off handsomely. It's a stretch of the imagination to think that one of Lieutenant Colonel By's men designed and built the open dish-dresser. But certainly, the man who built this early piece of Canadiana was a skilled woodworker who took much time and care in creating an object that must have had pride of place in that early stone house overlooking the distant Rideau River.

Catholic Church, Throoptown, ON, c. 1920, since demolished.

# 5
## Business With the Servants of God

I remember years ago hearing that an order of nuns planned to close and sell a large convent in the south end of Ottawa. Surely, I thought, an old building like that is bound to have all kinds of antiques. I decided to visit.

As a former Roman Catholic altar boy who dutifully served many a mass at St. Patrick's Cathedral on Kent Street in Ottawa, including one stint where I assisted at every single 7:00 A.M. service during Lent (a record that may stand to this day) I have more than a passing familiarity with the Church. In 30 years of collecting I have bought antiques and artifacts from the basements of churches, from the odd manse, and directly from priests, ministers, nuns, and the caretakers of religious buildings.

I vividly recall driving through one Eastern Ontario town where I saw several pieces of antique furniture on the front porch of a stately brick home next to a large stone church. I stopped and approached the front door and a gentleman answered. I asked about the items on the front porch, which included some quite nice antique oak furniture.

"Left over from a yard sale we had yesterday," the gentleman replied.

"Left over?" I said, shocked that anyone would leave behind the antiques I could see on the porch. "Is it possible to still buy today?"

"Sure," he promptly replied. "And I've got more in the house, too."

As it turned out, his home was the manse and belonged to the church next door until, during hard times, it had been put up for sale – contents included.

He gave me a tour of the home and in almost every room I bought one antique after another. The list included several pieces of furniture, lighting fixtures, paintings, hooked rugs, clocks, glass, and china. As we discussed the purchases, his family of small children ran about the house enjoying their free time.

Auld Kirk, near Almonte, ON, constructed in 1836.

When I left about an hour later, my truck was brimming with antiques and collectibles. One piece I recall from that haul was a fantastic oak armchair in original varnish and perfect condition. This was no ordinary armchair. The design was exuberant with shapes and curves everywhere and the oak in it was two inches thick. I've seen only one other chair like it in 30 years of collecting and it wasn't for sale. I sold my example in the group shop I was in at the time for about $300. Today, it would easily command $750.

While that day was a success, there were others much less so.

I have come up against some tough customers in my years of buying and selling antiques, but some of the toughest were nuns who looked like they were just about to head out the door to feed the poor when I happened along and asked them about selling any antiques they might own. In an instant, they would transform from meek and mild servants of God into hard-charging dealers ready and willing to take your last dollar, or close to it, for the oak hall stand in the foyer of their Mother House.

It always struck me as odd that these remarkably kind and generous women would freely sell the items from the convent, including religiously symbolic items. Clearly, however, the sisters knew when the time had come to downsize and move on. They are impressively efficient at getting the job done of closing and selling their facilities and returning to headquarters.

I can tell you without reservation though, that to this day, I'm sure no picker, (or altar boy) has ever knocked on a more imposing entrance than one in Ottawa South.

One approached the massive convent from a long laneway, then up a large set of stone steps to a pair of huge double oak doors; each one must have been eight feet high and five feet wide.

It was a daunting task for me to muster up the courage to approach those doors. It took two or three visits over a few weeks, sitting at the end of the laneway in the truck, muttering to myself. When the day finally came, I was one determined picker. I was going to take on those nuns come Hell or high water, so to speak.

I walked delicately up the stone steps until I stood in front of those imposing front doors. A huge brass door knocker hung from the right hand door. It was so heavy it took a fair amount of effort just to raise it up. I did so and let the thick circle of brass thud against the door. It echoed inside the building. The oak doors vibrated in protest beneath my hand. I waited. Nothing. I lifted the knocker again and let it fall against the door. Again, nothing. Then, finally, faintly, I heard the sound of footsteps approaching. The sound of the door mechanism engaging followed, and the door slowly swung partially open. A small nun in full habit stood before me with a rather stern look on her face.

"Hello Sister. I uh stopped today because I heard that the convent would be closing and I uh wondered if you might have any antiques or old things you might want to sell?"

I squeezed the truck keys painfully in my sweaty hands, waiting for her response.

There was a pause as Sister gazed at me rather critically, her left arm and hand still resting on the open door. Then, rather jauntily she replied: "Oh, young man, you're too late! We had a big sale here back a few weeks ago and sold all kinds of antiques. You should have been here for that!"

"Really," I said, my mouth agape.

"Oh yes, big, big sale. I'm surprised you didn't hear about it. Just about everything went. I'm just finalizing the sale of the altar items to a dealer on Bank Street."

"Well, is everything gone? M-m-m-maybe there's something left?" I stammered, trying to salvage a situation I knew was already lost.

"You're welcome to come in and look around," Sister said, pushing the door further open and beckoning me inside.

Sister took me on a personal tour of the huge convent building, which must have been four stories high. Up the stairs we went, into rooms, down hallways, through alcoves and more rooms. All the while, she happily pointed out the locations where various antique items had once stood, including pine cupboards, tables, and wash stands.

About the only antique item left was a gigantic oil painting that hung in the stairwell. I felt like a pipsqueak staring up the dark and foreboding canvas and its thick gilt frame.

"I believe that's staying with the building," she said longingly while looking up at the painting. "The new owners want it."

"I knew you were going to say that," I replied, staring up at the huge painting.

We continued the tour of the building. About 20 minutes later we finished and the good Sister chaperoned me back to the convent entrance. We said goodbye, I slipped out, and she swung the colossal oak door shut behind me. It closed with a decidedly solid thud.

I shuffled dejectedly back to my truck thinking the antique gods must have got the message wrong. What about all that good karma I earned being an altar boy? What about all those masses I served during Lent? 40 in a row! C'mon, I thought, that's got to stand for something! Alas, masses served, even 40 in a row, was apparently not the currency the antique gods knew or wanted that day.

Walking to the truck, I coined I a new phrase. "In antiques, if you're last, there's nothing left. Duh." I'm going to get that printed on cards and carry them with me forever!

It would seem that I have an attraction to convents. Some months later, after learning a Bible's worth from that one encounter, I turned my attention to another convent in the west end of Ottawa near my own home.

This convent had been in existence for many years and the Order had schooled young women and delivered other services to the poor and needy. The Sisters had also bought a mansion across the street as a residence for their Mother Superior. Time had moved on, however, and a For Sale sign had recently appeared on the lawn of the mansion. I expected one would soon be on the convent itself, too.

Muscling up my picker's nerve, I stopped at the convent one summer day. A Sister answered my knock, at a decidedly smaller front door than my earlier experience, listened to me politely, then showed me to an adjoining sitting room to wait for an audience with the Mother Superior. Before long,

Mother Superior entered the room, took a seat, and listened patiently while I repeated the purpose of my visit.

To her credit, Mother Superior understood my query right away and said that she would be willing to show me through the mansion across the street. We made arrangements to meet there in the afternoon and, true to her word, she was there at the appointed hour.

The home and its grounds took up most of the city block. The building itself was impressive, designed and built in the "prairie style" that was popular around 1910. Waiting patiently at the front door (I do a lot of that in this business!), visions of all kinds of antiques danced before my eyes. Surely the Sisters had owned the building for decades and likely bought it furnished. Certainly, there would be arts and crafts furniture, accessories, and lighting fixtures, maybe even a signed piece of Gustav Stickley oak furniture! I even flirted with the notion of perhaps purchasing the house and grounds. Now that would be the ultimate antique buy! Standing there at the doorway, I was practically giddy with anticipation.

A moment later, Mother Superior graciously opened the front door of her home and invited me into the foyer.

"Now, what would you like to see?" Mother Superior asked, acting very business-like.

"Perhaps you could just take me on a tour of the house and as we go through it, I will point out any items that catch my interest," I proposed.

"That sounds fine," she replied and turned smartly away toward the rear of the house. "Let's start down here."

Off we went on an extensive tour of what was then and still is an impressive heritage home. The downstairs rooms featured beautiful and exten-

From the "Manse" purchase, an elaborate solid oak arm chair, c. 1920.

sive oak trim and floors. A magnificent stained-glass window adorned the wall of the staircase and the shafts of coloured light streaming through it played over the oak bannister, the wall paneling, and staircase.

My first disappointment, of which there were to be many on this day, was the living room, which was sparsely furnished with only the basic comforts and certainly nothing antique. The contents of an adjoining sunroom proved equally disappointing. On we went, through the dining room – but no gracious quarter-sawn oak dining room table greeted us there. Next was a rather plain kitchen, updated unimaginatively in the 1950s. We climbed the stairs at the front of the house, Mother Superior setting a brisk pace. I held out hope that the second story or the basement would yield treasures otherwise stored away and forgotten. Again, disappointment. The upstairs rooms were spartan. Down we went to the basement. That space, too, had been cleaned out and we were met by only a bare, slightly musty smell and a few pieces of lumber lying in a stack against the wall. We climbed the stairs back to the main floor as Mother Superior chatted away in front of me and I followed behind, ever the optimist.

Any illusions I had about buying the house and grounds were quickly dashed when, half-way up the stairs, Mother Superior turned and looked back at me.

"Of course we were quite surprised when the house sold in one day," she said.

"Really," I gushed. "In one day?"

"Yes, we got $900,000 for it."

She went on to say that a successful local architect had bought the property and had plans to renovate and move in.

"Oh, I see. Well, good for you Mother Superior," my heart sinking the final few feet into the "you're not getting anything today" pit that we pickers know so well.

We finished the tour in an upstairs room where I finally saw and was able to purchase a small oak bookcase with glass doors, to which someone had unsympathetically glued semi-transparent decorative paper meant to simulate the appearance of leaded glass. It was a dismal failure and compared nicely to my equally dismal failure at finding any antiques in the house.

I later learned that the Order had bought the house from two brothers who were descendants of the man who had built the home. Apparently, during their tenure, they had, for one reason or another, sold off the contents of the house. When the Order came into possession of it, the antiques and special items were long gone.

I should mention that, while Mother Superior may have believed the story about the architect, I didn't. If pickers stretch the truth to buy an antique, real estate agents and developers routinely break it to bits. Sure enough, a few months later the land was subdivided, sold off, and redeveloped. Fortunately, the mansion survived. The sale of the convent building and land across the street followed shortly thereafter and the same developer called for the demolition of that graceful old building. After much uproar by the neighbouring community, the building was preserved and turned into a condominium. When a heritage building is destroyed, as so many in Ottawa have been, it is lost to us in the present. But more importantly, it is lost to future generations forever as they hold no memories of it.

Prior to the closing of the sale, the Sisters did stage a convent-wide sale of all of the contents. I walked through and had a look. It, too, was disappointing. Over the years, if the Sisters needed a piece of furniture, they simply asked their caretaker to build one. After many years and many requests, the convent was festooned with bookcases, shelves, and cupboards all constructed from plywood. There must have been some antiques there but they were not offered in the sale. Perhaps some other picker, better than I, scooped them up.

Business with the servants of God has not been entirely disappointing. There have been other convents and churches in my "picking" past. At one in Maniwaki, Quebec, I was able to purchase a number of antique items, including the case for a large grandfather clock.

Still, I would have thought all the good-altar-boy karma I earned as a child might have paid more handsome dividends in antique finds along the way. In any event, I had better save what little spiritual capital I have left for that day when I'll really need it!

A load of antiques in my 1983 GMC S15 truck. The late Edith Cathcart, my mother-in-law, is in the background – she also loved antiques.

## 6

# A Sign of the Times

Every once in a while, I would take a Friday off from my job as a public servant to devote to antiques. My routine never varied. I'd leave after breakfast and select a route for the day. One of my favourites was south down old Highway 16, the route that links Ottawa with Highway 416 at Johnstown on the St. Lawrence River. It's about an hour's drive at the lawful speed limit. But when you are picking, stopping, and talking to people, rummaging through barns, sheds, and attics, a normal one-hour drive can take all day. Once I reached old Highway 2, I would turn left or right and follow that route looking for antiques in and around towns and villages like Morrisburg, Cardinal, New Wexford, Prescott, Maitland, and others.

This particular Friday morning was a beautiful one in late May. I left Ottawa and traced my usual route south along old Highway 16, making several stops along the way. The weather was ideal, the people were friendly, but the search, as is often the case, produced nothing of interest.

I reached Johnstown and turned left onto old Highway 2 proceeding east. I soon noticed an elderly man mowing his lawn. His home was a modest older frame building set well back from the highway with a large barn behind it. Since he was outside working, I thought I would stop and ask him about antiques.

I pulled my truck onto the gravel road that ran adjacent to his property, drove to the end of it, and then turned and drove back to intercept him at the edge of the lawn. I pulled over opposite to where he was working and waved. He shut off the mower and walked the few steps over to my truck. I had already rolled down my window to talk to him.

"Hi. How are you doing today?"

"Good," he said.

"Grand day."

"That it is," he replied.

"I stopped to ask if you might have any antiques, anything old you might want to sell."

He considered my question for a moment. "Nope," he said. "I've got nothing like that."

"No old wooden cupboards, long tables, wash stands. Things made by hand in the old days."

"No. There's nothing around here."

I looked at his old house, which was visible behind him. "No antiques in your house that you'd like to sell?" The house looked like it could have antiques because it was certainly old enough.

"No, I don't think so. All those things are long gone."

We continued chatting about nothing important. Every few minutes, I would return to the subject of antiques.

"So, you don't have anything old you'd want to sell?" I asked for a third and then a fourth time.

"No, not a thing," he repeated, his arm resting against the side of my truck door. This man was sure of his answers!

Discouraged, I finally accepted that there was nothing for me there. After all, I had asked him the same question half a dozen times. It was time to go. This was just another in a long line of unproductive stops that day.

As I put my fingers on the ignition key to start the engine of my truck, he made one final comment.

"Come to think of it, I do have one old thing."

I turned my head slowly to look at him through the open window. His face was slightly whiskered, tanned, and lined from years of outdoor work. Though he was clearly in his late 70s or early 80s, his gaze as he looked at me through light blue eyes was clear and steady.

"What would that be?" I asked.

He paused. "It's an old sign."

"Oh, what type of old sign?" I sad, my interest suddenly piqued.

"An old sign used on a building."

"Well, would you show it to me?"

He paused and gazed down at the gravel road beside my truck and considered my question.

"I suppose I could show it to you."

"Great," I replied, pulled the keys from the ignition and got out of the truck.

The old fellow turned and marched across a wide expanse of lawn toward the barn that was set back from his house. Reaching the building, he opened a large sliding door and we entered. I followed him the length of the building, which was poorly lit, with only the daylight from the open doorway behind us and light seeping in through the cracks between the barn boards to illuminate the interior.

He went to the farthest corner of the barn where broken chairs and other detritus was piled up against the wall. Once there, he began pulling away the broken furniture, wooden boxes, and old hand tools until he exposed a flat object about three feet wide and two feet high. With a grunt, he pulled the sign toward him and placed it on its edge in front of me.

"Here's the old bugger," he snorted, breathing a little heavily from the exertion of revealing the sign and dragging it out of the pile. "What do you think?"

I bent down to examine the sign more closely. There was so little light it was difficult to see it in any detail. What I could see at first glance was that it was an oval with some sort of decorative metal work around its perimeter. On one side, I could make out the words "Riverview Restaurant" in white paint on a blue background. On the opposite side was more printing but in black letters on a grey background.

It was frustrating to examine the sign in the half-light of the barn.

"Would you mind if we took this outside so I can see it in the daylight?"

"No, I don't mind. Let's bring it out."

When you look for antiques for long periods of time, it's easy to become discouraged and your attitude suffers. Personally, I start questioning what on Earth I am doing wasting yet another day looking for antiques in areas where all kinds of pickers have gone before me. In the spring and summer, it can be hot, humid, dusty, and dirty. But all that discouragement and frustration – the feeling of wasted time, the heat and humidity – all of it drains away when you are standing in front of a potentially great find. One moment you're ready to quit, and the next moment brings the intoxicating feeling of great discovery. This sign, resting on the grass in front of me, could be one of my best finds of all time. I could feel it.

I knelt down in front of the piece. As I've said before, it's one thing to find an antique and an entirely different matter to buy it. I have found hundreds of exciting antiques over the years that I was unable to acquire.

I could feel adrenaline starting to course through me. I had to remain calm. Getting overly excited about an object can easily destroy a potential deal.

"Yeah, it's an old sign all right," I said. "Would you like to sell it?"

He paused, both of us staring at the sign, which was propped up between the two of us, my hand resting on its edge to keep it from falling over.

"I dunno, make me an offer."

There was another short pause while I considered my next step. I had to make an offer but it had to be just the right amount.

"How about $25 dollars?"

He gave the figure some careful thought and to my astonishment said, "Sure. That sounds good."

I took the $25 dollars from my pocket and passed it to him without a word. Then I picked up the sign and headed for my vehicle, where I placed it carefully in the bed of the truck. I turned and waved to the old man. He nodded his head, returned to his lawn mower, and resumed cutting the grass.

I turned back to the sign again for another long look. It was then that I realized why the sign had two different names on it. The blue side of the sign was actually artist canvas, which had been fastened by a series of upholstery tacks spaced about half and inch apart and running around the entire edge of the sign. There was enough space between the edge for both the decorative ironwork and the upholstery tacks. Clearly, the last owner had repurposed the sign sometime in the 1950s for his restaurant – *The Riverview*. But rather than paint directly on the sign, he had put the image he wanted on the canvas, thereby saving what was underneath. I peeled away a portion of the canvas, and sure enough, in original condition underneath, just like the opposing side, was the name, *"Peters Inn"* written by hand in heavy black script. When the sign was originally made, it was two sided and meant to hang from the building in such a way that travellers would see it from both directions. Whomever had modified the sign for the *Riverview Restaurant* knew they were going to mount it flat to the wall so only one side had to be visible. The opposite side would be placed against the exterior wall of the restaurant and would never be seen.

I jumped in my truck and headed back to Ottawa. Arriving home, I immediately took the sign to my basement workshop, where I slowly removed all of the tacks holding the canvas to one side and finally revealed the sign in its original state. What I now owned was a tavern or inn sign that dated to the early 1800s and was quite possibly older than that. It was made of pine, roughly three feet wide by two feet high, and perhaps two inches thick. The decorative ironwork running around the entire oval was hand-forged in a pattern of half-circles with an iron point between each of them. Other than a good dusting, the sign needed no other restoration and once I cleaned it, I brought it upstairs and propped it up on the fireplace mantle in the living room to admire.

When they come onto the market, antiques often follow a predictable path. An object comes in at the bottom of the market when a picker finds it or an individual owner offers it to a local dealer. That picker or dealer may sell it to another dealer, who in turn sells it to another. This will continue as long as the next dealer up the chain feels there is still money to be made. Objects therefore tend to migrate toward veteran dealers who can command higher prices. At the end of the process, when the object leaves the market and disappears into a collection, the final price paid is considered to be the market price for that object.

As highly desirable objects come back onto the market from collections, the market has moved forward in terms of price, because by then it is even more difficult to find that particular type of item. Typically, a piece will go back through the same process, passing through various dealers' hands, until it reaches another, final customer.

It's not difficult to buy a piece inexpensively, sell it, and make money. The challenge comes in buying a piece at a high price and still making money when selling it. For example, selling an object with a market value of $5,000 for $1,000 is not difficult but selling that same object for $5,000 when you've purchased it for $4,000 takes more skill, nerve and experience. You've got a margin of $1,000 with which to work. That might seem sufficient, but when you start haggling over price that margin can be whittled away pretty quickly.

Some collectors never sell an item. One collector who toured me through his collection several years ago told me that when he first started to collect he sold an item. Afterwards, he was so upset with himself for doing so he vowed that day to never sell another. And he didn't. He has since passed away and his family had to do what he could never do: dispose of his collection.

For someone with a modest income, the return of what I paid for a piece and, hopefully, a profit, lured me into dealing in antiques. As much as I loved some of the things I found and bought, I knew I had money invested in them, money I wanted back. So, while I continued to buy, there always seemed a good reason to sell.

Older, more experienced dealers made a point of calling me to see what I had found and I used to call them too. They knew a great deal more than I did and, on many occasions, I sold things I probably shouldn't have sold or sold them for far less than they were worth. Veteran antique dealers often take advantage of new, less knowledgeable dealers and pickers.

Veteran dealers stay close to new pickers because they know that inexperienced pickers will find things and be unaware of their market value. They can buy items relatively inexpensively and make a good profit. As pickers gain experience they increase their prices, find higher-end dealers to whom they sell, or both. Indeed, some pickers sell their finds to a specific dealer only.

If you're a picker, "the quick flip," according to some, is the best way to operate. By selling an object quickly you turn your money over and it is then available for the purchase of the next item. Your money, and overall profit, builds through volume and repetition. However, as I've found, you have to accept the fact that in selling an item early, the sale price will be far less than it's worth on the retail market. While you still make a profit, the dealer you've sold it to will make an even bigger profit, as he or she has a higher overhead and a higher echelon of collectors.

Travelling and working with another picker can be productive, as well as a great way to learn. I was never comfortable with that arrangement and although I tried it a few times, I preferred to search on my own.

There is a hierarchy in the antiques business. As I've mentioned, experienced dealers can often obtain a much higher price for an object because they have a reputation for selling that quality of item in that price range. An unknown dealer will find it difficult or impossible to obtain the same price because he or she lacks the reputation for handling antiques at that level. So, even if you know that a piece has a much higher market value, as a dealer you may not be able to obtain that price because you don't have the reputation for handling such an item. In fact, some collectors will buy only from certain dealers because they trust only their judgment and the pieces they handle.

An hour or so after I had cleaned and displayed my new find, the doorbell rang. It was a dealer I had known for sometime. I forget now whether it was an arranged visit or if he just dropped in. He came into the house and immediately spotted the sign on the mantle and wanted to buy it. I resisted his offers and we chatted about other things. It wasn't long before he left.

The doorbell rang a second time. This time is was another dealer I knew and with whom I had done much business over the years. As I recall, he was there to pick up something he had purchased from me the week before. He, too, immediately noticed the tavern sign on the mantle. "Wow, where on Earth did you get that?" he asked, standing in front of the sign and admiring it.

"I picked it this afternoon." I said proudly.

"Locally?"

"Yes, not far from Ottawa."

"I want to buy it."

"No," I said sternly, "It's not for sale."

"Why not? I can use this."

"Because I just got it. I want to think about it."

"Look, I'm doing the Christie Classic show this weekend. I need something special for it. This sign would be perfect."

"No, sorry."

"Listen, I'll give you $600 for the sign. I'll take it to the show and if I sell it I'll give you even more than that!"

"No, no. I don't want to sell it."

With that, I walked him to the front door and out on to the porch. He started walking down the laneway. As he reached the rear of his vehicle, he turned and yelled back at me.

"Are you sure? I'll give you $600 right now.

"I stared at him at the end of the laneway. Neither of us spoke.

"Well?" he said.

I paused again. Then replied: "Oh, all right then, I'll sell it!"

The mercenary side of me had won out. I had little invested in the sign, and I could not resist the handsome profit. I think he was more surprised than I was and he wasted no time rushing back to me. He took $600 cash out of his wallet and gave it to me. I walked back to the house, picked up the tavern sign from the mantle, and brought it to the front door. He took it carefully from my hands and walked quickly to his vehicle. He wasn't taking any chances on me changing my mind. In a moment he was gone.

I learned one important lesson that day: if you don't want to sell an antique, do not show it to a dealer!

Word travels fast in the antique business. A couple of days later, I heard through the grapevine what happened to my tavern sign at the Christie Classic show. Apparently, an Ottawa-area collector whom I know well was also selling antiques at the show. He saw the dealer unpack the sign and place it on a table in his booth. He immediately asked the price and bought the sign. He then placed it in his booth where, so the story goes, an American collector saw it and wanted to buy it. Although he was rebuffed several times, the collector persisted and toward the end of the day was able to buy the tavern sign. Word has it that the price paid was in the order of $2,000.

The Peters Inn tavern sign was found in a barn similar to this.

When I next saw the dealer to whom I had sold the piece, he didn't know that I knew what had happened. He told me he had sold the sign for just over $600 so there was no extra profit to share with me. For some reason, I didn't challenge his version of events. I simply accepted his story, knowing it was false, and let it go at that. I knew I had made a serious mistake when I sold the sign to him originally and nothing, certainly not a few hundred dollars, was going to change that. I couldn't blame him for pressuring me to sell the sign either. He was simply doing what antique dealers do: trying his hardest to buy an object he coveted. Ultimately, he was successful. I succumbed to his pressure, just as the elderly gentleman who sold the sign to me had accepted my offer on that beautiful spring afternoon so long ago.

There are some antique objects that remain fresh in your mind long, long after they have left your possession. The image of the *Peters Inn* tavern sign remains in my mind to this day. For a few short hours I owned what was, and perhaps still is, the best trade sign ever to come out of Eastern Ontario. It's gone now, but the memory of that day is always with me. From time to time, I think about it when I am on the road, when I come round a bend and see an old barn, a shed, or an outbuilding and wonder if that's the resting place of my next spectacular find.

**Author's Note:** Since completing *Folk Art in the Attic*, I learned, assisted by Fraser Lashinger and the Grenville County Historical Society, that Peters Inn was located in the Village of Johnstown, Edwardsburgh Township. In 1846 the Inn was owned by Stephen Peters and "was a small operation consisting of two rooms and three beds for hire." For information about heritage stone buildings in the Township, refer to: *The Stones of Edwardsburgh*, by Sandra H. Robertson (Grenville County Historical Society 2008).

The cupboard from Glengarden, Ottawa, ON. c. 1880 (Acquired 1997)

# THE ANTIQUE THAT WASN'T FOR SALE

I f you like antiques, chances are good that you also like heritage homes and buildings. I love walking into a heritage home. The feeling of time and history that emanates from an old home is remarkable. On occasion over the years, I've taken advantage of open houses held on weekend afternoons to view old homes put up for sale.

On one particular day, I happened to be in an area known as Ottawa South. This older part of the city is bounded on the south by the Rideau River, on the north by the Rideau Canal, on the west by Bronson Avenue, and on the east by Riverdale Avenue. The many heritage homes located there are mostly fine red brick structures built in the early 1900s. The *Billings Estate*, a national historic site dating from 1829 and one of Ottawa's oldest homes, is nearby.

On a little side street called Barton, just a few blocks from the Rideau Canal, is a beautiful red brick Victorian home with fancy gingerbread trim and porches painted a creamy yellow. Above the front door in wood letters is the home's name: *Glengarden*.

Glengarden was built by the Poaps family around the turn of the century and the family lived there for generations. It was originally a dairy farm with an adjacent apple orchard situated well outside the City of Ottawa. By the mid 1980s, when the house was offered for sale, the municipal boundaries had expanded far south of Glengarden and the home was surrounded by many newer ones built over the intervening years.

One day I happened to notice For Sale / Open House signs on the property and took the opportunity to walk through the house. A friendly real estate agent welcomed Joan and me and we walked through the first floor of the house, admiring the high ceilings, beautiful woodwork, and the hand-plastered Victorian details in the dining and living rooms. I strolled

Bank Street Bridge in Ottawa South, c. 1920. From the City of Ottawa Archives, CA024415.

to the back of the house. A door off the kitchen led into a wooden shed-like structure built on the back of the house. I stepped into the shed, which was virtually empty except for a large, flat-to-the-wall cupboard situated against the right-hand wall.

Since the rest of the house was empty it was surprising to see this antique cupboard sitting in the shed. Looking at it more closely, I noticed several interesting features about the cupboard.

Although it had a straight front, the cupboard was divided at the middle by two drawers. It boasted an interesting, wavy cutout across the base and a built-up cornice. I also noted that it was constructed entirely of ash or elm and sported its original varnish with white porcelain knobs. A hardwood cupboard is less sought after than pine, although some examples made by German and Polish immigrants of Renfrew County are prized by collectors.

This cupboard was likely made for the house around the turn of the century. The square nails in the backboards also suggested an early date, perhaps 1875. The hardware used in furniture is helpful in dating an antique and antique collectors are quick to inspect that particular feature.

Hand-forged nails are recognizable from their irregular heads, which at the time were literally fashioned by the hand of a blacksmith. The heads of these nails are rough and uneven and are an indicator of a piece of furniture made in the first quarter of the 19th century. Square or cut nails are so called because they were literally machine cut from a sheet of iron. The heads of these nails are uniform. Furniture with square nails dates from 1825 to 1860. Finally, wire nails with round heads indicate a date around the turn of the 20th century.

Collectors are excited to find hand-forged nails in a piece of furniture, while round wire nails weaken the appeal of an item because it often means the piece was constructed after 1900 and outside the 100-year bracket, which is the standard used to qualify items as truly antique.

Collectors also carefully inspect the hinges on the doors of antique furniture because the type of hinge and whether they are made of forged metal, cast iron, steel, or brass helps a collector estimate the date of construction.

The manner in which the lumber is sawn is also a general indicator of age. When viewing the back of an antique cupboard, for example, straight saw marks on the surface indicate the boards were made using the "pit saw" method; that is, the log was positioned over a trench with one man in the trench and one man above using a manual saw. Round saw marks are proof that a powered circular saw, a later invention, was used to manufacture the lumber.

Advanced collectors and dealers are also familiar with furniture designs from various time periods. While features used often overlap, sometimes by many years, they are useful in dating antique furniture.

In all, the Glengarden cupboard was impressive, and while not a total crowd pleaser, it was still an interesting local antique and one that I wanted to own. However, there was an obvious problem and it was staring me right in the face – a cardboard sign someone had made and taped across the upper doors. In large black letters, the sign read: Not For Sale.

Well, that's disappointing, I thought to myself. Here, you find a nice cupboard and it's not for sale! I took a final look at the piece, turned away dejectedly, and made my way back into the kitchen to rejoin Joan and the real estate agent, who were chatting casually when I approached.

"Joanie," I said, with a note of resignation in my voice. "There's quite a nice cupboard out there in the shed. Too bad it's not for sale."

Just then the real estate agent responded. "You mean that big cabinet against the wall?"

"Right. That one."

"Oh," she said, "I don't know if it's for sale or not. I just got tired of everyone asking me so I made that sign and taped it to the front."

"Well," I replied, it's quite a nice piece. I really like it."

"Do you want the phone number of the owner of the house? You could call and find out if it's for sale."

"Sure," I replied. "I'd appreciate that."

She walked over to a small table, wrote down a phone number on the listing sheet, and handed it to me. We thanked her, ended our visit, and walked outside to the car. I put the sheet of paper in my pocket and made a mental note to call the number later that evening.

After supper, I remembered the piece of paper. I placed it beside the phone and dialed the number. A man answered.

"Hello," I said. "I was at an open house on Barton Street today and noticed an old cupboard in the back shed. I was wondering if it might be for sale?"

"No, I don't think it's for sale," the man replied.

Oh well, I thought to myself, I guess that's it. So much for that cupboard.

After a pause, he said, "But actually, I don't own the cupboard. My nephew owns it. Did you want to call and ask him?"

"Yes," I said. "For sure, I'll give him a call."

"Just a second and I'll get his number for you."

With that, he proceeded to dictate the phone number, which I wrote down next to the one given me by the agent. I hung up and dialed the new number. A young man answered and I repeated my request.

"Hi. My name is Shaun. I was at an open house today in Ottawa South and noticed an old cupboard in the back room. I understand you own the cupboard and wondered if you might be interested in selling it."

There was a pause on the other end of the line and I readied myself for the same negative answer.

"The old cupboard. Sure, I'd sell it. How much would you give me for it?"

Aberdeen Pavilion at Landsdowne Park, c. 1900. Members of the Poaps family would surely have attended events here. Photo from the City of Ottawa Archives, CA007687.

It took me a few seconds to think about it.

"I'll give you $500 cash."

"Sold. It's yours."

We made arrangements for me to pay him and to stop by the house and pick up the cupboard, which we did the following day.

When I got the cupboard home, my brother Scott came by to look at it. Like me, he admired the craftsmanship and attention to detail that had gone into the construction of the piece.

To this day, I often wonder why the real estate agent offered the phone number of the owner to me and not someone else who had asked earlier in the day. Perhaps it was because I was the last in the line that day. I'll never know. Sometimes, with antique hunting, that's just the way it happens.

As it turned out, I had limited space in my home for another case piece of furniture. And, since he liked it so much, I sold the ash cupboard to Scott and to this day it resides in his home in Ottawa, where it continues to serve a useful purpose for his family, much the way it did in its original home of Glengarden.

The Toonerville Trolley c. 1930.

# THE TOONERVILLE TREASURE TROVE

T he rise in popularity of the humble yard sale coincided with the start of my career searching for antiques and folk art.

Yard sales, also known as tag sales, garage sales, or lawn sales, first came to prominence, at least for me, in the early 1980s. I will also include estate sales in this chapter, although those events typically involve selling the entire contents of a house and not superfluous items, which is the rationale for a garage or yard sale. Further back in time, the public auction was the chosen method to disperse a household's goods and chattels. It was also a way for friends and neighbours to purchase keepsakes of the family whose farm or home and contents were being auctioned.

These days, on Saturdays throughout the spring, summer and autumn seasons, it is difficult to drive through any urban Ontario neighbourhood without seeing multiple signs for yard sales. In fact, the phenomenon has become so popular that entire neighbourhoods stage mammoth one-day community garage sale events in which hundreds of families participate.

The *Great Glebe Garage Sale*, held in Ottawa's Glebe neighbourhood, encompasses dozens of city blocks and attracts so many people that the entire neighbourhood is practically grid-locked with cars and pedestrians for the entire day on which it is held each year. Suburban antique dealers rent laneways in the area for the day to participate.

The difference between garage sales held 25 years ago and today is that the garage sale used to be popular with middle-aged couples and seniors who were downsizing and needed to disperse unwanted furniture and other items in preparation for a move to smaller quarters. Much to the delight of collectors and dealers, these sales often included antiques and collectibles. Now, younger families use yard sales to purge unwanted items including toys and children's clothing. Sales held by younger families typically do not include

The Great Glebe Garage Sale, Ottawa ON, 2012.

antiques and collectibles. Unfortunately for dealers and collectors, the latter type of sale is far more prevalent today and many a frustrating Saturday can be spent visiting one sale after another without ever seeing an antique.

But in years past, garage sales have frequently produced some astonishing antiques and collectibles for me. It was not uncommon to stop at a yard sale and see the entire contents of a home, including many pieces of antique furniture, lined up on the edges of the laneway and spilling onto the adjacent lawn. On many occasions, I filled my truck with desirable antiques and collectibles, all purchased at a single garage sale!

The average person staging such a sale does not know the value of the antiques or collectibles in their home, some of which may have been sitting in the basement or attic for years. They hold the sale in order to get rid of things, and antiques and collectibles are put out along with everything else. Dealers and collectors now know that yard sales can produce valuable finds, and they are the first to descend on the sales – sometimes as early as 6:00 A.M. on a Saturday.

Many antique dealers scan the local newspaper and Internet sites for yard sales, which by necessity always include the address of the sale. They stop by the home on the Thursday before the sale to ask about any antiques. More often than not, the homeowners are happy to sell them – they see it as an opportunity for an advance sale. Of course, advance selling is frustrating for all the other would-be buyers who arrive on the appointed date and time expecting a chance at buying antiques and collectibles, only to find them gone.

On many occasions this has happened to me. If the antiques aren't there, I automatically conclude that a dealer or collector has already purchased them. I can't tell you how many times I've been told, "Oh, the antique furniture? Some guy came around on Thursday afternoon and do you know, he bought everything!"

Despite these frustrations, I have found and purchased some exciting antiques and collectibles at yard sales; a few occasions stand out in my mind.

One Saturday morning I was in suburban west-end Ottawa, having stopped at a yard sale. What looked promising from the roadside turned out to be another disappointment. I stood at the entrance of the garage feeling quite discouraged, when suddenly just a few feet away, the neighbour activated his inside garage door opener and, with much creaking, the metal door slowly lifted upward, revealing several tables filled with antiques and collectibles.

When I am first on-the-scene at a garage sale, I know I have to act quickly. I have, by my estimate, two minutes at most to look over the contents of the sale, find the antiques and collectibles, and purchase them before other customers arrive.

In this case, I started at the front left side of the garage where a makeshift set of several shelves had been set up to display the items for sale. I quickly noticed that the majority of items on every shelf were antique or collectible, including desirable pieces of china, glass, porcelain, and other objects. Equally surprising was that the antiques were priced inexpensively, between $1 and $2. I looked to my right and saw more sets of shelves along the interior of the garage also filled with interesting objects.

Knowing that time was of the essence, I gestured toward the first shelving unit and announced: "I'll take everything on these shelves." The owners were only too happy to oblige. I moved up the wall to the next shelving unit. "And, I'll take everything on these shelves, too."

I next turned my attention to a large table set up in the middle of the garage, which was filled to the edges with more items. I quickly started selecting antiques and collectibles from the table and passing them to the couple. "I'll take this, and this, and this, and this. These as well."

Soon I had gone over the entire contents of the garage and purchased everything I wanted. The couple kindly wrapped the items and put them in large boxes for me. Several minutes had elapsed and there were still no other buyers in sight.

The small pine armoire, Ottawa, ON, c. 1870. (Acquired 1995)

At this point, the couple asked me if I would like to see a china cabinet in the house that they had for sale. I readily agreed and they showed me into a room that contained a very nice, curved glass china cabinet in mahogany on cabriole legs with ormolu mounts and other decorative trim. The cabinet needed restoration but it was an attractive piece even in its present condition.

"Did you have a price in mind?" I asked.

"How about $100?" replied the homeowner.

"Yes, I'll take it."

We made arrangements for me to come back later in the day to pick up the cabinet. In the meantime, I returned to my vehicle and started loading the various boxes.

It was then that the first of other buyers walked up the laneway. The first to appear was an acquaintance and a fellow dealer. As he passed by my car, he asked. "How is the sale, Shaun?"

"Oh, not bad," I said. "I bought a few things."

I stopped at another yard sale in the late 1990s, staged under the cover of a carport of a west-end Ottawa home. Initially, I didn't see anything of interest on the large table that had been erected in the laneway to display the items for sale. Then I noticed a small fishing reel in the middle of the table. I was struck by its colour – the side casings of the reel were a bright green, which contrasted vividly with the chrome parts of the reel. It was in perfect condition. On the housing of the reel I found the manufacturer's name: Arjon. Beside the reel sat its leather case and a small container, which housed a set of small tools to clean and oil it. For $4, I quickly picked up the reel and handed the owner the money.

Later that day, I sat down at the computer to do some research on this little gem of a reel. It didn't take long before I discovered that Arjon was one of several Swedish manufacturers of fishing reels, and their products are highly sought after and prized by collectors the world over. The particular reel I purchased at the garage sale was made around 1950 and was one of the models that was most difficult to find. At the time of my purchase, eBay was very much in vogue as an effective means of selling antiques and collectibles. I put the reel up for auction on the site and it very shortly sold for much, much more than I had paid for it. I discovered later that the purchaser was the President of a Japanese fishing tackle manufacturing company.

The whole notion of value and what is a fair price to pay for a collectible is an interesting topic. At first, when your knowledge is limited, paying the asking price or close to it seems fair. Neither you nor the seller is really aware of the market value for items. You can easily lose money. But, as your knowledge grows, with it grows your understanding of market. At a certain point your knowledge is far greater than the seller's. The dilemma for some buyers is paying an asking price when they know that an object is worth more – sometimes a great deal more. On occasion, I have offered to pay more than the asking price which, not surprisingly, pleases the seller to no end.

When there is no asking price, the challenge is to arrive at a figure that is acceptable to both the buyer and the seller. Most frequently, however, the seller is at a disadvantage. Because there is money involved and because antiques and collectibles have value, this interplay between buyer and seller is always present.

One Saturday, I was driving back to the city after a day in the Ottawa Valley spent looking for antiques. Nearing home I saw a sign at the end of a street indicating an estate sale was underway nearby. I turned and drove up the street, stopping at a small bungalow with several cars and trucks parked out front. I found a parking space and hurried into the house. The upstairs was full of people examining various items. Nothing caught my eye, so I walked through the kitchen and went into the basement. There were several people down there as well, milling about looking over the various tools displayed on the workbenches. In an adjacent room, I noticed a small pine armoire against a wall. Although there were people in the room, no one was paying any attention to the armoire. I approached a woman who was clearly in charge of the sale.

"I was wondering if that little cupboard is for sale?" I asked.

"No, it is not for sale," she said pointedly.

Disappointed but not surprised, I turned and started to retrace my steps when I noticed another lady in the main room of the basement. She was obviously a sister of the woman who had just turned me down. Without thinking, I turned to her as I walked by and said, "Is the little cupboard in the other room for sale?"

"The little cupboard. Sure."

I was taken aback for a second but quickly asked, "Well, how much do you want for it?"

"How about $25 dollars," she replied.

"Sure," I said. "I'll take it."

I quickly handed over the money, and with that she headed back into the furnace room with me close behind. We arrived at the cupboard.

"Here," she said. "You take an end and we'll get this out of here."

As we lifted the little cupboard, people reacted with surprise. More than one person commented, "Hey, I thought that cupboard wasn't for sale."

Amid the grumblings and jeers, we quickly walked the cupboard to the stairs, up and out the side door, and down the laneway to my truck. Once loaded, I headed for home, quite happy that I had thought to ask the question not once but twice.

Sometimes, if you're lucky, you'll discover a yard sale before the event takes place. Such was the case when an out-of-town meeting I attended finished early on a Friday afternoon. I had just pulled out onto the highway and started my trip home when I drove by a laneway filled with various objects. I wasn't sure if someone was simply cleaning out the garage and temporarily storing belongings outside, or if they were preparing for a yard sale. I parked and walked into the laneway to find the homeowner.

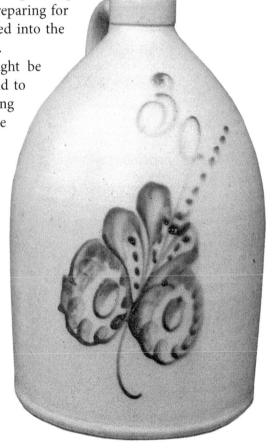

"Hi. It looks like you might be preparing for a yard sale," I said to a woman who was busy hauling a piece of furniture out of the garage.

"That's right, we are. Tomorrow, actually."

"Would you mind if I looked around?"

"Not at all. Have a look!"

I had already noticed several antiques lying around the laneway and on the lawn, although the garage and the home looked relatively new.

"You seem to have quite a few antiques but this looks like a new house," I observed.

"Oh, she said, actually it's an old house that we renovated. A lot of these things were in the house when we bought it."

Decorated, salt-glazed stoneware, Ottawa ON, c. 1860.

59

I motioned toward a pine wash stand. "Are you interested in selling some things now before the sale?"

"For sure. What would you like to buy?"

That was all the invitation I needed. I proceeded to walk up to the various antiques, pointing to them and making offers, which she readily accepted. After the first pass, I loaded the antiques I'd purchased into my truck and went back for a second look. This time, I wandered into the garage only to find several more desirable pieces of antique furniture. I continued to make offers and the homeowner continued to gladly accept them. By the time I left, about an hour later, there was only enough room in the truck for me to squeeze in for the drive home.

I waved goodbye and thought: if I had glanced left instead of right, I would have missed the opportunity of buying this truckload of wonderful antiques and collectibles.

On another occasion, I had stopped at a local delicatessen to buy some items for the weekend. As I stood at the counter waiting to pay the cashier, a small boy approached. In his hand he held a sheet of paper, which turned out to be a flyer advertising an upcoming garage sale his family was planning for the weekend. He was with his mother, who was in the shop next door distributing the same flyer. While he waited patiently to talk to the storeowner to ask permission to post the flyer, I casually glanced down at the sheet in his hand. The word "antiques" appeared prominently in the heading.

Looking down at him, I said, "I see you're having a garage sale on the weekend."

"Yes, sir," he replied.

"And your family is selling antiques?"

"Yes, sir. My mom is coming in now. She can tell you about them."

His mother walked to the counter and I asked her about the antiques.

"Yes, we're moving and we have several antique items we want to sell."

"I buy antiques," I replied.

"Well, would you like to come over and see the things?"

"Sure. When would be a good time?"

"You can come now if you'd like. We're on our way home after this."

We made arrangements to meet at their house just a few short blocks away. As agreed, I arrived a few minutes later and the woman showed me into the house. The antiques in question turned out to be mostly small items, primarily plain stoneware crocks. There were about 15 or 20 of the crocks in various sizes gathered in a group on the floor in the middle of the room. One piece caught my eye. It was a three-gallon, salt-glazed, stoneware jug with a large cobalt blue decoration painted on the front. Decorated stoneware is highly sought after by collectors and this was a very nice example.

"Well, of all these items, I'd like to buy the large one in the centre," I said.

"Sure. Make me an offer."

"How about $75 dollars?"

"Yes, that will be fine." she said.

I gave her the money, took the stoneware jug outside, and placed it carefully in the front seat of my car.

It's not often that you go to the delicatessen and arrive home with cold cuts *and* a decorated piece of Canadian stoneware!

One of my more memorable yard sale finds was at a sale in the west end of Ottawa on a street adjacent to where we were living in 1983. An older woman was selling various possessions. I wandered up the laneway to examine the items on tables and in the garage. It was early on a Saturday morning and I was the only person at her sale.

In the middle of a large table set up in the garage, I noticed an old toy made of tin. I leaned over to the centre of the table and picked it up for a closer examination. The toy was an odd-looking train engine with a conductor or driver standing on a platform at one end. The name *Toonerville Trolley* was printed in large letters on the sides of the vehicle. I knew right away that this was a vintage toy and bought it immediately for a few dollars. I learned later that it was first made in 1922 in Germany by Nifty and known in collecting circles as a "tin litho wind-up toy". The toy was based on a popular comic strip created by Fontaine Fox and first published in the *Chicago Post* from 1908 until 1955.

After purchasing the toy, I chatted with the woman for a few minutes.

"If you like toys," she said, "I have more of them in the attic. They belonged to my son when he was growing up."

"I'd like to see them." I replied quickly.

"Today's not a good day because I'm looking after the sale here and can't take the time. But why don't you call me in a couple of weeks?"

I wrote down her name and number and agreed that I would call back and make the arrangements to get together.

The summer wore on and my professional life took a rather sharp turn when I was offered a new job in Pembroke working for the County of Renfrew. The rest of that summer was spent packing up the apartment, house hunting in Pembroke, and moving up the Valley to start the new job. In the midst of all that commotion, I forgot about the Toonerville toy lady and didn't make the call to visit with her.

A few months went by. We had settled nicely into a new home in Pembroke. It was only 90 miles from Ottawa but it was a full-scale move with all that that entails. I think it was in October when I again came across the name and number of the Toonerville toy lady in a note pad I kept for follow-up antique calls.

To facilitate matters, since I was out of town, I asked my brother Scott if he would call and make the appointment to see the toys. I called the woman and she agreed to show Scott the attic contents that coming weekend. With the arrangements made, I went about my business in Pembroke and forgot about it.

The following Saturday afternoon, my phone rang in. Scott was on the other end of the line, calling from the lady's house.

"Shaunie. I'm calling from the house." His voice sounded hushed and excited.

"Hi Scottie. How's it going?"

"God, Shaunie, you wouldn't believe what's in this attic!"

"Why, what is it?" I asked expectantly.

"This lady has *everything* her son had growing up. There's every toy, every baseball card, every hockey card, every board game, everything! The attic is full of it."

"Wow. That sounds incredible."

"It is. And, get this, she wants to sell it all! What should I do?"

"Well, buy it!" I said, sounding, I'm sure, far too casual for Scott's liking.

"Yeah, but there's so much stuff! And I don't know what to offer."

I paused to think about it. For some reason the figure of $200 popped into my mind. "Make an offer of $200 then."

"Are you sure? OK, that's what I'll do."

We hung up the phone. A few hours later Scott called me with good news.

"Shaunie! Offer accepted. I got it all!" he said, also noting that he had moved the entire contents of the attic a few blocks over to where he was living.

"That's great news, Scotty! Joan and I are coming to Ottawa this weekend so I'll come by your place to see the stuff."

On Saturday, we arrived in Ottawa and I drove to Scotty's house and parked in his laneway facing the double garage at the rear of the property. Scotty saw me arrive and came out the back door to meet me.

"I've got everything in the garage," he shouted from the back porch. I was excited to see what he bought but also knew we'd have to spend at least an hour or two unwrapping and getting the various items out of boxes so I could see them.

Scott reached for the handle low down on the right hand garage door, pulled on it, and the white door swung out and up, letting the light reveal the interior.

Nothing could have prepared me properly for the sight of what was in that garage. There, spread out on several tables, was the haul from the attic. Scott had gone ahead, unpacked everything, and carefully placed the items neatly on the tables.

"Oh, my God! Look at this. It's unbelievable!" I whispered completely taking aback by the scene in front of me.

Scott stood back and grinned impishly. "I thought you'd get a kick out of this."

It's been 30 years since Scott pulled that garage door open. I still get shivers when I think of the scene. Everything the Toonerville lady's son had as a young boy, on up into his teenage years and beyond, was now in that garage. There were hundreds if not thousands of vintage hockey cards and baseball cards, most of them in complete sets. This included dozens of *Bee Hive* hockey photographs. These photographs were free give-aways from the St. Lawrence Starch Company of Port Credit, Ontario from 1934 to 1962. There also must have been over a 100 classic toys from the 1940s and '50s, including dozens of classic Dinky Toys.

Scott had done a masterful job of organizing and displaying all of the items and the tables literally took up the entire interior of the garage. We spent the next hour or so going through everything. It was one amazing revelation after another.

Over the following year, he and I gradually sold most of the items from the garage, although he did hang on to a number of the toys for many years afterwards. As the items were sold to collectors, time moved on and the thrill of that exciting find faded. But there's no question that it was one of the most memorable finds of my collecting career, even though it was Scott who actually closed the deal on the Toonerville treasure trove.

Crucifix by Arthur Sauvé, Maxville, ON, c. 1955. (Acquired 1994)

# 9

# SEARCHING FOR AN ARTHUR SAUVÉ

I t was while reading a book on Canadian folk art that I first came across
the name of Arthur Sauvé (1896-1973). From Maxville, Ontario, Sauvé
was a wood carver who created a range of interesting items including small
works of animals, cases for musical instruments, religious items, shelves,
picture frames, and whirligigs. His attention to detail and meticulous carving ability set his work apart from many other artists who work in wood.

I had heard rumours about a carving he made of a hockey game in
progress with the rink, players, and rink boards all incorporated into what
must be a remarkable piece of work. According to rumour, it apparently
turned up at a yard sale in the Cornwall area around 1990 and was sold to
a dealer shortly thereafter. (I have since had an opportunity to see a Sauvé
"hockey game" in the collection of the Canadian Museum of Civilization).
His "man on the bike" whirligigs are in a league of their own.

Although I attended many auctions in the Maxville area, an example
of Sauvé's work had never been offered for sale at one of them. Always a be-
liever in the power of advertising, I decided on another method to unearth
one of his carvings. I wrote a small classified advertisement indicating that
I was interested in buying pieces of his work. I placed the advertisement in
a couple of the local newspapers in the Eastern Ontario area near Maxville,
sat back, and waited for a reply.

About a week later my telephone rang and when I answered a woman's
voice on the other end of the line responded. "You're looking for Arthur
Sauvé's carvings?"

"Yes, I am."

"I have one, if you're interested."

"I appreciate you calling. What do you have?" I replied.

"We have a crucifix that he carved."

"Sure, I'd be interested in that item. When could I see it?"

We made arrangements for me to drive down to Maxville on the following weekend. I recall that the woman brought the crucifix out of the house as I waited on the steps and put it into my hands so I could look at the piece more closely.

Until that point, I had seen only photos of Sauvé's work in reference books. To hold one in my hands and to see the craftsmanship and artistry evident in his work was an amazing feeling.

Sauvé often incorporated chip carving into his work. It is a process whereby the artist builds up layers of thin wood, the edges of which have regular small indentations carved out of them. In this case, the crucifix had been formed by several layers of chip-carved pieces of wood. The figure of Christ was fully carved, painted, and affixed to a cross. In all it was about 20 inches in height and likely dated to about 1950.

The asking price was reasonable and I purchased the crucifix on the spot. I was satisfied that my advertisement had worked. What I didn't know was that it was still working!

Another week or so went by and the telephone rang again. A young man on the other end of the line asked, "Are you the person looking for carvings by Arthur Sauvé?"

"Yes, I am."

"Well, we have one that is for sale."

"Great! What do you have?"

I fully expected the caller to describe an animal carving or perhaps another crucifix. I was taken aback by the response.

"It's a man on a motorcycle and there are these blades up above and when they turn in the wind, the man peddles and his legs move."

I was momentarily speechless with excitement.

"Right! Yes! I am very interested in that piece. Where are you and could I come to see it?"

As it turned out, the young man was calling on behalf of his aunt who owned the whirligig.

"Well, you could come Saturday if that suits you."

"Saturday is fine." I hastily replied.

On the following Saturday morning, Joan and I made the drive to a small town near Cornwall. We drove into the laneway of a small brick bungalow, and Joan waited in the car while I walked up to the side door and rang the bell.

A few moments later, the young man to whom I'd spoken on the telephone came to the door and invited me in. After introductions and shaking hands he turned and said, "We have it downstairs in the rec room. Follow me."

The basement room was paneled and nicely finished. He turned right at the bottom of the stairs and walked toward a small bar at the end of the room. There, sitting in the middle of the bar, was, unmistakably, a "man on the motorcycle" whirligig by Arthur Sauvé.

I tried to remain calm and composed. All I could think about was purchasing this great piece of Canadian folk art and taking it home to my collection. We examined the "bike" together. It was in near perfect condition, and the artist had even signed and dated the piece with carved letters from bone or ivory, spelling out, "*A. Sauvé 1962*". It was a stunning piece of folk art. The only thing left for me to do was to buy it.

I forget now whether the young man asked for $300 or if I made the offer, but I handed him the cash and he handed me the whirligig. I carried it with one hand on the wooden column that supported the bike and the fan above, and one hand gently underneath the bike. I emerged from the side door carrying the piece that way and walked to car watching as Joan's eyes widened with surprise.

Later that day, when we had returned home, I took the time to have a much closer look at the whirligig.

Sauvé must have been at the peak of his carving prowess when he created it. He made this masterpiece in 1962, some eight years before his death in 1970.

The main component of the carving is a man (with a hat, of course), riding what appears to be a motorcycle. However, since the man peddles when the blades turn in the wind, it has more the action of a bicycle. (There may have been hybrid-type motorbikes in the early 1960s, a bicycle with some sort of engine mounted in the frame that the rider pedaled initially and then engaged some sort of clutch mechanism to activate the motor). What Mr. Sauvé wanted us to observe, and what he so successfully created, are the astonishing details of his carving.

I am certain that Sauvé knew he was making a decorative piece of art. The form was a whirligig but it was never meant to spend a day outside in the elements. The relatively fragile structure would not have survived past the first year. Mechanically, his design was impressive but I doubt the wind would have ever turned those blades despite the fact that there were ten of them.

Arthur Sauvé's "Man on a Motor Bike," 1994.

Other artists have made whirligigs, and there is no end, it seems, to the possibilities of what one can design to react to the wind. Most whirligig designs are relatively simple – a bird whose wings rotate in the wind, a man chopping or sawing wood, a woman milking a cow, an individual rowing a boat – these are all examples of designs that collectors have seen many times over.

What sets Sauvé's whirligig apart from most is its sheer complexity: a man riding a bicycle with the man's legs pedaling and the pedals and the wheels of the bicycle turning simultaneously. Other artists I'm sure have attempted this type of whirligig design but I doubt anyone has executed it to a comparable level of skill and creativity.

There are essentially four components to the piece. The motorbike, the man riding it, the wheel-like structure at the top of the piece designed to catch the wind and provide the power for the pedaling action, and the square column of wood that supports these components.

The details that Sauvé included in his creation were remarkable. The rider's legs are articulated at the knee and hip. Other significant details include coloured tail lights, brake cables, a license plate with the year "1962" and the abbreviation for Ontario "ONT" (with the "N" backwards.) The tires were carved from single pieces of wood, each with 14 spokes. The tread of the tires was meticulously carved. A kickstand, headlights and fenders made from thin wood formed into semicircular shapes over the wheels completed the incredible details of the piece.

Sauvé didn't paint the whirligig. Although another known example he made is painted, its execution was less sophisticated. With the version I acquired, it's almost as if he didn't want anything to detract from the mechanical achievement of the work. Painting the parts different colours might have been a visual distraction. Interestingly, the Canadian Museum of History (formerly the Canadian Museum of Civilization) has another version of the "motorbike" whirligig also by Sauvé. It was made in 1949, some 13 years

Detail from Arthur Sauvé's "Man on a Motor Bike."

before the one I found. While it shares some similarities, the overall construction seems crude compared to the 1962 version. The wheels, for example, are circles of wood with the spokes simply incised into the surface. In the later version, Sauvé carved the wheels, including each individual spoke.

Folk artists like to use all available spaces in their work. They feel that a blank space is wasteful or that the viewer will be cheated if a space is left undecorated. In this case, Sauvé could have left the backside of the square wooden column blank. After all, who would look at the back of the piece, and especially at the back of the structural column on which the components were mounted? But, Sauvé adorned even that space. Measuring only two inches wide and roughly three feet in length, it would have been a unique challenge to conceive of a decoration to suit this space. True to his creative genius, he solved the dilemma by carving a long, narrow, decorative snake, which he affixed to the surface of the rear column. He even added costume jewels to the eyes of the snake. The other three sides of the column also received attention, with small wooden diamonds mounted a few inches apart along each of them.

Sauvé also made sure to identify this masterful work. He mounted a small wooden plaque to the vertical support column with the words, "*WIND MB MADE BY ARTHUR SAUVE, MAXVILLE, ONT, 1962*". (It's my assumption that he abbreviated the phrase Motor Bike into the letters *MB*).

I owned the whirligig for several years. I even offered it for sale at the *Ashbury College Antique Show* in Ottawa and at the *Bowmanville Antique and Folk Art Show*. There were no takers and I happily took the piece home and displayed it prominently in my office. From my desk, I had only to turn to my right slightly to gaze at one of the most amazing pieces of folk art I will ever own.

In the late 1990s, Joan and I decided to purchase a cottage property in the Gatineau Hills an hour north of Ottawa, on a lake where my family had vacationed for many years. I needed money to complete the transaction and decided to sell antiques to finance the purchase. Although I hated to do it, I knew the Sauvé whirligig would fetch a good price and give us a head start for the cottage purchase. I contacted a well-known and respected dealer who came to my home to look at the whirligig. It took only a few minutes to agree on a price and he left with the whirligig. He in turn offered it for sale at the *Bowmanville Antiques and Folk Art Show* and I believe it was sold during the show. What would the value of that piece be today? I think a figure of $7,500 would not be unrealistic. Perhaps more.

I have not seen the *Man on a Motorbike* since I sold it 15 years ago, but I am sure it must be the centrepiece of someone's collection. Whoever they are, they must enjoy owning what is, in my opinion, one of the truly great and iconic pieces of Canadian folk art ever created.

At my first Bowmanville show.

## 10

# DOING BOWMANVILLE

"Bowmanville" – one single word that speaks volumes to any collector of Canadian antique country furniture and folk art. It refers to the *Bowmanville Antiques and Folk Art Show*, an event held every Easter long-weekend in Bowmanville, Ontario. In 2013, the show celebrated its 40th year. There, in the local community centre, some 35 dealers gather each year to display some of the finest country furniture and folk art they can offer, much of it of museum quality, the majority of the pieces in original paint.

I've participated as a dealer in the show a few times over the years. It is a unique, if somewhat intimidating, experience because you are surrounded by some of Canada's legendary dealers and collectors. Several of the Bowmanville dealers have been doing the show for many years. One in particular (Smiths Creek Antiques of Port Hope, Ontario) has participated for every one of the show's 40 years. I first participated several years ago, scurrying around for months in advance, finding and buying objects that I thought were of Bowmanville quality.

Over time, usually many years, experienced collectors and dealers develop an "eye" – the ability to look at an object and know with certainty where that piece sits on a scale of quality. A mental checklist of attributes automatically kicks into gear at the first sight of an antique or piece of folk art.

High-end dealers in Canadiana have the advantage of having handled hundreds, if not thousands, of antiques in every category. Doing so has trained their eyes and minds to recognize and to differentiate the mundane from the great. Many, many times over, a less experienced antique picker will unearth a desirable Canadian antique and sell it quickly, only to discover afterwards that the item is far better than they had originally thought. This has happened to me on several occasions. It will happen to anyone who ventures into the buying and selling of antiques.

However, a collector who finds a fabulous Canadian antique, frequently through a dealer, an auction, or private sale, acquires the piece and knows it will never be sold. Or, it will only be sold in order to upgrade the collection with an even better example.

A wise man once told me that you should never resell a piece of real estate you've purchased for at least a year. His theory was that one should allow for a period of time to reflect on the purchase and to assess the market, which may have shifted further in your favour in the intervening 12 months. The same theory can be applied to the purchase of antiques. If you think you've found something great, put it aside and reflect on it. Conduct research, use the acquisition as an opportunity to learn and understand why the piece you've just found is "great," discuss the piece with fellow collectors, and compare the object with similar pieces in reference books. Doing so will help train your eye so that recognizing quality in a Canadian antique becomes instinctive. You'll also avoid making the mistake of selling too soon! Of course, if you're "picking" and depend on sales for your livelihood, you'll have no choice but to sell fairly quickly. The upside to the quick sale is that you'll have money, including a profit hopefully, to buy more antiques.

As your ability to assess an antique improves, you may start to find your earlier acquisitions wanting. Some objects won't score well on the quality checklist and at that point you may want to dispose of them or trade up for better quality items. After all, few people have unlimited physical space to store and display, for example, pieces of Canadian case furniture. So, trading up in quality and selling a poorer example of, say, a cupboard, often becomes the only option. That said, I know collectors who, after filling their homes with Canadian antiques, keep right on collecting and fill barns, sheds, and other buildings with items that they can no longer fit into their homes. The passion for collecting Canadian antiques runs deep in some collectors. They can't stop. I know the feeling well.

As my first Bowmanville show approached, I needed more items of quality and, as dealers will often do out of necessity, I turned to my personal collection to provide them. I remember selecting two items in particular. The first was one of the best folk art paintings I've ever owned.

Like many of my finds, the acquisition started innocently when I responded to a classified ad in a weekly newspaper advertising antiques for sale. Nothing in particular caught my attention in the wording of the advertisement, but where there is a group of antiques being sold there is always the potential for a significant find. It was late in the afternoon in the autumn of 1989. I picked up the telephone and dialed the number.

"Hello. I'm calling about your ad in the paper."

"Right, that's my ad," replied the voice of an older man on the other end of the line.

"Can you tell me what kind of antiques you're selling?"

"Well, there's some furniture, an oak ice box, smaller items, glass and china."

"Is it possible to come and see the things?"

"Sure. No problem. You can come tonight. There are other people coming to see the stuff."

"How about 7:00 P.M.?"

"That'll be fine."

I arrived at a modest suburban bungalow a few minutes before 7:00, parked my truck in the laneway, approached the front door, and rang the bell. A moment later, a middle-aged man welcomed me warmly into his home.

After introductions and some brief small talk, he motioned toward a door behind him. "Well, you'll want to see the antiques. I have them downstairs."

He turned, took a few steps, and opened the door. I followed him down to a rec room that was overcrowded with modern and antique furniture, including the oak icebox and unframed artwork stacked in piles and leaning against the wall.

The icebox was a good one in fine condition and inexpensive. I bought it on the spot for his asking price of $200. I asked if I could look through the paintings in the stack leaning against the wall immediately beside the icebox.

"Yes. Go ahead and have a look. They're all for sale."

I slowly thumbed through the pile of paintings and noticed one by a listed Ottawa artist. I made him an offer for all the paintings and he happily agreed to the price.

"Do you have other things for sale down here?" I asked as we wandered to the right of the staircase into a room at the far end of the basement.

"Well, possibly. What are you looking for?"

At that point, I noticed a large packing case about four feet square leaning up against the wall. It was made of wood with straw-like stuffing visible through the narrow openings between the wooden slats that made up the case.

"What's in the packing case? I inquired.

"It's a painting. It came down in my ex-wife's family. It's been sitting here for a long time."

The Baril painting prior to restoration.

"Would you mind if we opened the case and had a look?"

"No, I don't mind. Go ahead."

He reached over to a nearby tool bench, retrieved a hammer and passed it to me. I knelt in front of the case and carefully pried off two of the slats, enough so I could separate the packing material and see something of the painting. I could only glimpse a few square inches but it was enough to know that this was an interesting piece of folk art. What I managed to observe of the painting was the windowed, dark brown front door of a farmhouse with green wood clapboard siding adjoining it.

I looked no further and stood up.

"Interesting painting," I said to him. "Can I buy it?"

"Yes, I'd sell that."

We quickly agreed on a price. Just then the doorbell rang.

"I'm expecting other people to look at the things. But they're late. They can wait."

We concluded our business and I gathered up the items I purchased, including the painting, which by then I had carefully removed from the packing case. We carried everything up the stairs onto the first floor. Whoever had been ringing the front door bell had given up waiting and left. We went back down to the basement and together brought up the icebox and put it in the back of my truck.

When I returned home, I ignored everything else in the truck and brought the painting inside. I placed it carefully on the dining room table and took a close look. There before me, as I had hoped, was a superb folk painting of a graceful, small farmhouse complete with brick chimneys, gabled windows, a summer kitchen extension, and a white carriage shed at the rear with a set of arched double doors. The home featured details like brick chimneys, a lightning rod, and three gabled windows on the roof. It wasn't dated but I was sure it was created about 1840. Family members and itinerant artists often painted images of family homes and farms. Before photography, it was a method of creating and preserving an image of a farm that could be proudly displayed in the parlour for everyone to see.

The artist had also painted white wooden-railed fences in front of the house and the adjoining field. A mountain range was in the background and an orange tinted sky suggested an evening sunset. The painting was housed in a beautiful hand-made pine frame, and could be easily removed from the frame simply by turning two hand-carved, small wooden latches on the reverse, which held the stretched canvas in place. An artist's signature, "Baril," was visible in the lower right hand corner.

There was, however, damage to the painting. A two-inch square area of paint on the bottom half of the front door was missing. But I knew a conservator who could "in paint" that and match it perfectly. I had the work done the following week and hung the painting proudly in a room at home. I never tired of looking at it. Clearly, as the painting indicated, this was a prosperous and well-managed farm with proud owners who were meticulous about its care and maintenance. With the Bowmanville show fast approaching, I earmarked the painting as an object that would be featured in my booth.

Along with the farm portrait, I took another folk painting from my collection – a "seagull" portrait by the Nova Scotia artist Joe Norris (1924-1990). While not as well known as Maud Lewis (1903 – 1970), Norris was a major Canadian folk art talent of the highest order. At that point in time, he was rapidly gaining attention as an important folk artist. His paintings of maritime life displayed immense natural artistic talent. While the seagull portrait was relatively small, he also painted works on a much larger scale and decorated the surfaces of furniture with various multi-coloured scenes. His "starry night" series of canvasses, depicting men and women in horse-drawn sleighs swishing down the main streets of Nova Scotia villages, are extraordinary. Each star in the dark sky above the village is painted individually and with the utmost care. I have a Norris "cove" scene in my personal collection and it occupies an important place in our home and always will.

So, these two paintings – the Quebec farm by Baril and the Norris seagull portrait – along with several other precious antiques and examples of folk art, went with me to my first Bowmanville Show in 1993. My younger brother, Sloan, accompanied me. It was good to have a member of the family along because it is stressful setting up at a show like this. Sloan and I moved the items in from the truck and set them up on display in the booth that had been assigned to me on the floor of the community centre where the show was being staged.

The Bowmanville Show is eagerly anticipated and collectors from across Canada line up for several hours in advance so they can be first to see the items on display. In its early days, before being moved to the community centre, the show was held in a local motel. Dealers set up their objects for sale in motel rooms and customers would flock from room to room, upstairs and down, examining and purchasing the antiques on display. That was before my time as a collector or a dealer. It must have been organized chaos!

The show opened that year with the usual rush of collectors and I enjoyed several sales within the first hour. I had the farm portrait sitting on an easel on the left-hand side of the booth. The Norris seagull portrait was displayed on the booth partition wall nearby. I had put what I thought was a substantial price on the farm painting, $1,400 if I remember correctly. I don't remember anyone paying much attention to it until a young lady walked up and stood in front of the work. I approached her and we exchanged a few words about the painting. She continued to stare at the painting and then, much to my surprise said: "I'm buying it and giving it to my brother as a gift for his house."

With that, she took out a chequebook and paid me. A few moments later, with the painting wrapped and held safely under her arm, she disappeared into the crowd of people in the aisle in front of my booth.

The sale of an antique, even in an antique show bustling with people, is a personal transaction between the seller and the buyer. No bells ring, no lights flash. A decision is made, a cheque is written or cash exchanges hands, a receipt is given, and it's done. The dealer stands, often alone in his booth, while the crowd continues to walk by. I've never quite adjusted to the rather abrupt manner in which these objects leave my possession. One

Looking outward from my booth at the Bowmanville Show, April 2012.

minute they are mine; I am still admiring them although they sport a price tag. The next minute, they are sold and gone. As a dealer, you are pleased to have the money in your hands, but as a collector, you hate to see these special objects leave. Before long, the money has been spent and you are left with an unsettling feeling of regret. You have the memories of owning the object, perhaps a photograph, but that's all.

Compare that to owning a special item and keeping it safe in your home, where it is admired by family and friends for years. I know these are inanimate objects but after a while they do become like old friends, albeit silent ones. Every once in a while, when I pass by an object in my collection, I'll stop and examine it yet again. I'll admire the craftsmanship and attention to detail that went into its creation. Better yet, the memories of its acquisition come flooding back as I recall finding the item and buying it. In a busy life with careers and family, these moments are fleeting, but they are at the heart of the collecting experience.

After the sale of the farm painting, another woman entered my booth. Before long, she was standing in front of the Norris seagull portrait. Again, we exchanged a few words about the painting. Again, I had placed what I thought was, at the time, a substantial price on the work: $450. Some collectors know what they want and can reach a decision quickly. Others will torture themselves for hours, and longer, before committing to a purchase. This individual was solidly in the first camp. After just a few moments, she declared, "I'm taking it, and it's going home with me to Barrie."

I wrapped the painting and off she went. Of course, I have never seen those two folk paintings again. Dealers and collectors often repurchase items and return them into their collections. If I ever have the opportunity, I would happily buy back those two paintings in the blink of an eye.

Dealers often say that your show is made or not in the first few hours. This is especially true of Bowmanville. By the end of the Friday evening there were many empty spots in my display area. I had a few more sales the following day. Late Saturday afternoon came, and my first Bowmanville experience was over. Along with the other dealers, I packed up the remainder of my items, loaded them into my vehicle, and Sloan and I drove back to Ottawa.

That first Bowmanville experience was 20 years ago. Recently, via the Internet, I made a sale of an item to Dr. Martin "Marty" Osler of Toronto – a veteran dealer of the Bowmanville Show. He has since become a good friend and I eagerly anticipate a visit to his offices in Toronto, where he displays many great examples of Canadian antiques and folk art. In the course of one of our conversations, he encouraged me to again set up at the event. In typical fashion, I waffled and put off the decision until finally, in an email, Marty wrote emphatically to me: "*Do Bowmanville!*" So, some 20 years after my first time, I found myself again setting up as a dealer for the 39th edition of this venerable event, and again the following year.

Doing Bowmanville again after nearly two decades was exciting and somewhat nerve wracking. But antique dealers are welcoming and friendly. As I was setting out my antiques and art for the 2013 show, a dealer I know stopped by to say hello.

"Things are going well," I said. "But you know, I find getting set up for this show stressful."

"Shaun," he immediately replied, "I've been doing Bowmanville for 37 years and I *still* find it stressful!"

Later on at the dinner held for dealers on the Friday night after the first day of show, I had the good fortune to sit with several dealers whom I've known, through business dealings, for many years. On my right was Peter Baker, one of the most knowledgeable and experienced dealers in Canada in Quebec country furniture and folk art. Across the table sat Clay Benson, a veritable legend in Canadian country furniture antiques. On my left was David Field, an extremely knowledgeable dealer of country furniture and folk art. To converse with these individuals about antiques is an enriching experience and one of the side benefits of participating in the show.

Many of the things I found and offered for sale at the Bowmanville Show this year are gone to new homes and collectors. The objects that didn't sell now reside again in my collection and I am glad to have them there. It was exciting searching and shopping in advance for the show. And, of course, the show itself is a marvelous display of Canadian antiques and folk art. As a collector, it is a wonderful experience to walk around the show before the event opens to the public and quietly examine the objects on display so carefully presented by the dealers.

On the drive home from this year's show, I took an alternate route to the 416 along some of the secondary highways. Driving east, it wasn't long before I saw an old shed-like building behind an older home. I slowed and turned into the laneway. My search for objects for the next Bowmanville Show had begun.

Clowning around at the Bowmanville Show, 1993.

"Sleigh Ride to Church", Maud Lewis, 1962. (Acquired 2002)

# THE WORLD OF MAUD LEWIS

I t was the mid 1980s when I first saw a painting by the late Maud Lewis of Marshalltown, Nova Scotia. The small, vividly colourful works of art she created, depicting scenes of everyday life in and around the coastal villages of Nova Scotia, have a remarkable naive charm. The fact that these works of art were created by an individual who suffered much personal hardship and ill health in her life makes them that much more impressive.

Given her personal challenges, one would not be surprised if her creations depicted sterner subjects with moody atmospheres and somber colours. But that is not the case. Lewis' paintings brim with joy, innocence, and the simple beauty of the life and times in which she found herself as a child and as an adult, despite that life often being harsh and cruel.

My first acquisition of a Lewis painting was the result of a bulk purchase of folk art, which I described in Chapter 2. This particular painting featured a horse-drawn cart and driver in a country landscape. Looking to recover my investment in the collection, I included the Lewis painting in a sale of Maritime folk art that I organized in a group shop in Ottawa. A close friend and his wife came to examine the various items in the sale. I stood beside him as we both admired the colourful works of art displayed in front of us. After a moment, he turned and quietly said to me. "We'll take the Maud Lewis painting."

It was my first sale out of the collection and I was happy to see the painting go to friends. But afterwards, as was often the case, I regretted selling it. I made up my mind there and then that I would search for another work by the artist to replace the one I had sold.

Some months later, my wife and I stopped at an estate sale near the Rideau Canal in Ottawa South. We walked through the home and looked at the various items for sale, none of which interested me. The antiques were all from the Victorian era and certainly nothing in the country, Canadiana line. I returned to the front hall of the house rather dejectedly to wait for Joan, who continued to look at the items for sale. Just inside the front door an older woman was sitting behind a small table. She was collecting money from customers at the sale. I leaned against a wall opposite her.

"How come you aren't buying anything?" she inquired of me.

"There's nothing here that interests me," I responded rather abruptly.

"Why, what are you looking for?"

That's a question I've heard many times as a collector. Often, I choose not to really answer it and brush the question off by saying, "Oh nothing in particular." Other times, I'll actually answer the question honestly as I did on this occasion.

"Well, I collect country furniture and folk art." I said flatly.

There was a long pause and the woman sorted her papers on the table. She looked back in my direction.

"Folk art? I have a painting at home by Maud Lewis."

"Do you?" I replied immediately. "Are you interested in selling it?"

"I could be but it's not here in Ottawa."

"Where is it?" I asked.

"I live in Cornwall."

"I'll be happy to drive to Cornwall to see your painting."

She wrote her telephone number and address on a piece of paper and handed it to me.

I agreed to phone her at the beginning of the following week to set up an appointment to see the painting. A week later, Joan and I drove to Cornwall. We arrived at a small, well-kept home on a suburban street and the woman welcomed us. After seating us in the living room, she said: "I keep the painting in a trunk. I'll go and get it."

She returned a moment later, carrying a pillowcase with a flat object wrapped inside it. "I keep it in this pillow case in a trunk. I don't know why but I've never had it framed or hung it on the wall," she said, extracting the painting and handing it to me.

The painting was in perfect condition. It was a winter landscape depicting a couple in a sled crossing a bridge. The road on which they travelled led to a church in the background. It was signed *Maud Lewis* in the lower right hand corner.

"It's beautiful," I said, holding the painting in my hands. "Have you got a price in mind for it?"

"I'm asking one thousand dollars," she said rather sternly.

I thought about it and glanced briefly at Joan, who was sitting beside me on the couch. "Will you accept a cheque?" I asked.

"Yes, I will."

"Then we'll take it."

I made out the cheque and we left shortly afterwards with the painting held carefully under my arm. We drove home to Ottawa satisfied with the purchase, knowing that a worthy replacement had been found for the Lewis painting I had sold in the show.

There is strange phenomenon associated with antiques. You can search for years and not see an example of a specific item and then all of a sudden come across one. A week later you'll see another one. Perhaps a month will go by, and you'll find another, and then nothing more again for several years.

Not long after acquiring the replacement Lewis painting, I happened to visit an antique dealer/picker in Ottawa with whom I had done business in the past. He showed me a small Maud Lewis painting that had turned up at a local flea market the previous week. It was a winter scene similar to the replacement Lewis I had purchased in Cornwall. In the image, a horse-drawn sleigh, in the foreground, approaches a small yellow covered bridge. Another sleigh or cutter is seen in the distance. A small red church with a white spire stands in the background, presumably the destination for these winter travellers. It was a very desirable painting and I wanted it. We discussed price and arrived at an agreement. For $200 cash and a piece of furniture (a nice wash stand if memory serves me), I took the small Lewis painting home.

As is common among collectors, I often attend estate sales, which typically include antiques and collectibles. I made a point of informing professional organizers of estate sales that I was buying paintings by Maud Lewis. They promised to let me know if any of these paintings turned up in their sales. It was several months after my last Lewis acquisition when I received a telephone call from an estate sale coordinator who told me that there were two Maud Lewis paintings coming up for sale in her next event. She agreed to let me see them in advance and I visited her at a home in the suburbs of Ottawa where the sale was scheduled to take place the following weekend. She greeted me warmly at the front door.

"Hi Shaun. Come in. The paintings are in the living room."

We entered the living room and sat down adjacent to each other on the couch. In front of us on the coffee table were two early Maud Lewis paint-

Another Maud Lewis purchase: "Butterflies and Blossoms". (Acquired 1995)

ings. Both were cove scenes about twelve inches square. In one, seagulls fly energetically overhead while two small fishing boats rest at anchor in a tiny harbor. In the left foreground, the wall of a shed on stilts is covered with red shingles.

In the second painting, a schooner approaches the entrance of a coastal harbor while another sailing ship plies the water in the middle foreground. A village of houses hugs the distant shore and again, sea gulls fly overhead. Both paintings were signed "Lewis" in the bottom right-hand corner. They were beautiful examples of her work and as soon as I saw them I wanted them.

"These are very nice little paintings," I said. "How much are you going to ask for them?"

At the time, the market for Lewis paintings was nothing like it is today. She was a well-known folk artist, particularly in Atlantic Canada, and less so in Ontario, although many tourists from Ontario had stopped at her house in Marshalltown in the 1960s and purchased work directly from her. Often, they took photographs of her house as a further memento of their trip out East. Over the years, I have been shown several of these photographs and I have two in my files that were taken around 1960 and given to me as part of the purchase of paintings.

"Shaun," she said, "We've put a price on these of $750 dollars for the pair."

"And, would you sell them to me before the sale?" I asked.

"Yes, I'd sell them now."

I paused to think about it. By today's standards that figure might not sound like a great deal of money. However, 25 years ago, it was. I continued to stare at the little paintings. It was the moment that occurs so frequently in the hunt for objects you desire. In the search for antiques and art, you'll often find something important at a yard sale for little money. The decision to buy is not influenced by the money required. It's trivial. On other occasions, you search and search hoping to make a discovery, knowing full well that you are going to have to pay more than you would like. At the time, we didn't plan for the purchase of antiques and art for our collection. Somehow, we just absorbed the cost into our ongoing spending.

I took a breath. A light rain was falling and I could hear the drops hitting the sill of the living room window to my right.

"I'll take them." I said.

I took out my chequebook, placed it on the table beside the paintings and wrote out the cheque. We carefully wrapped the paintings and I drove home, happy with the purchase, but also uncomfortable knowing that the family budget had taken a major hit.

In 2002, I placed a classified ad in a Toronto community newspaper, indicating that I was looking to buy paintings by Maud Lewis. I made arrangements with my sister, Sharon, to use her Toronto phone number in the ad. There wasn't much of a reaction, but as Joan often says: "All it takes is one!" About two or three weeks after the ad ran, Sharon received a telephone call from an individual indicating that they had both a Maud Lewis and a Joe Norris painting for sale. The price for the Maud Lewis was $1,000 and the Norris was priced at $5,000. I followed up and made arrangements to see the paintings the next weekend. I was given an address off Yonge Street in downtown Toronto. I finished the work week in Ottawa and headed down to Toronto for the weekend. My niece, Bianca, said she wanted to accompany me. So, off the two of us went to the address, which turned out to be an older high-rise apartment building just off Yonge Street in the downtown. We parked, walked into the building, and took the elevator up to the 11<sup>th</sup> floor. The hallway had a fairly low ceiling and the air was ripe with cooking smells from the various apartments.

"This is starting to feel like a drug deal," I said, straight faced, to Bianca, who smiled back at me as we exited the elevator, turned right, and walked down the hallway. We knocked at a door and a young woman opened it.

"We called about the paintings?" I said expectantly.

"Sure. Come on in," she said.

We soon found ourselves in the middle of the living room. The young woman went to the nearby dining room table, picked up a painting, and brought it to me. I immediately knew that I was looking at a genuine Maud Lewis painting. The subject was Maud's cat, Fluffy. It was a portrait of Fluffy with tulips bordering the left and right sides of the canvas. It was signed by the artist in the lower right hand corner. (In her earlier works, Lewis signed only with her surname. In later works she began signing with both her first name and last name. She had a habit of using upper case letters for the "M" and "A" in her first name. Also, she placed the "E" in her last name slightly on top of the lower bar of the "L". The "S" is always tipped to the right. These are characteristics I always look for when examining one of her paintings). Because she and her husband often handled the paintings while the paint was still wet, they often left fingerprints near the edges – another tell-tale sign of authenticity. Lewis frequently painted on a wall-board material that had a light green colour. I turned over the painting and was relieved to see the green tinge there.

"The painting belongs to my mother," the young lady said. "I'm selling them for her."

"Right," I said. "And there's a Joe Norris, too?"

"Yes, I have it here," she said, turning and walking over to the chester-field, which was against the window.

The Norris painting was done on cardboard. All I can remember was that there was a young boy depicted in the painting. It was unframed and quite a crude work considering the elegance of Norris' other paintings. The price of $5,000 struck me as completely unreasonable and I wasted little time in dismissing it.

I turned back to the Lewis painting, which was still in my hand.

"I like the Maud Lewis painting. I'll buy it." I took $1,000 cash out of my pocket and handed it to the woman. We thanked her, and Bianca and I left and drove back to my sister's home in north Toronto. Once in the door, I propped up the painting on the mantle over the fireplace and it stayed there for the rest of the weekend until we took it home to Ottawa and hung it proudly in our home, where it has remained ever since.

I didn't know it then, but my small classified advertisement was going to produce further results. Some time after purchasing the "Fluffy" portrait in Toronto, I received a telephone call from a woman in London, Ontario who said she had two Lewis paintings to sell. Apparently, a relative had seen my advertisement, clipped it out of the paper, and given it to her. She kept the clipping for several months before deciding to call. Naturally, I was excited to discuss the paintings with her. As it turned out, she had "ordered" the paintings from Maud Lewis in the early 1960s. We discussed price. She had placed a figure of $2,500 on each painting, which was roughly the market price for them at the time.

She described both paintings in detail. One was a winter scene in which two deer look down over a valley with a small village. The other was also a winter scene with a man driving an ox pulling a large load of logs. As it turned out, the owner's daughter was coming to Ottawa for a conference and we agreed that she would bring the paintings with her so I could have the opportunity to see them in person.

On a rainy afternoon in the autumn, I made my way downtown to one of the major hotels. The owner's daughter had placed the paintings on the bed in her room. As soon as I saw them, I wanted them. There was no doubt they were authentic. After examining them closely, I put them back on the bed, looked up and said to the woman.

"I'll pay $3,500 cash for the pair."

"I'll call my mother right now and ask her," she replied.

With that, she walked over to the desk by the window and dialed her mother in London. A short conversation ensued while I continued to look at the paintings. A moment or two later she hung up the phone.

"My mother says that will be fine."

"Great!" I said and took the cash out of my pocket. I counted out 35 100-dollar bills and placed them on the bed beside the paintings.

She gathered up the money while I placed the paintings back in the paper wrappings in which she had transported them. We shook hands and I left.

I can distinctly remember walking out of the hotel and across Queen Street to where I had parked my car. I don't know if every collector feels this way, but frequently after a major purchase, I often question my decision. "Should I be spending this amount of money on art?" "Should I be spending it now?" "Aren't there are other more important things that we need?" A dealer knows that he or she is going to sell the objects they purchase as soon as possible; not so with a collector. The collector plans to keep his or her acquisitions forever, or at least for a very long time. So, that sets up a "keep" versus "sell" tension with which I am very familiar.

At the start of a career, the debutante dealer tends to sell everything he finds. It's a question of survival and earning an income. Over time, as you become more successful, you can afford to keep some of your acquisitions and build a personal collection. It's difficult to be both a collector and a dealer, yet just about every dealer I know has an impressive collection of antiques, art, or both.

While I have had the opportunity to buy a number of Maud Lewis paintings, on more than one occasion I have missed out on a purchase. About 15 years ago, I got word through the grapevine that a well-known dealer in Eastern Ontario who handled more formal antiques (silver, brass, fine mahogany furniture, and the like) had recently acquired two Lewis paintings. I immediately called his shop and enquired about the paintings. I remember him saying that they had suffered some damage from being nailed directly to the wall, a situation that is quite common with Lewis paintings. Apparently, the individual had simply torn them away from the walls without removing the nails, so the panels on which they were painted had narrow tears through them at the corners where the nails had been. The damage was annoying but it sounded minor and I knew could be repaired.

"Have you put a price on them?"

"They are $2,000 for the pair," he replied emphatically.

"I'd like to come and see them."

"They'll be in the shop at 10:00 A.M. tomorrow," he said loudly, as if making the announcement on a public address system.

I had done business with this dealer before, including selling him some nice items at an antique show in which we both participated. I had hoped, based on our past business dealings that he would put aside the paintings and give me first opportunity at them. Obviously, that wasn't going to happen.

"Fine," I replied, "We'll come out to see them."

The next day was Saturday and, given that the drive would take us about 45 minutes, I planned on arriving at his shop around 11:00 A.M. The day dawned beautifully and after a leisurely breakfast and enjoying the Saturday paper, Joan and I set off for the dealer's shop.

"Deer Overlooking the Valley", Maud Lewis, 1963.

We walked in at 11:00 A.M. sharp. The dealer was standing behind the counter with two customers in front of him. I approached, and to my dismay, saw right away that the young couple had in their hands both of the Lewis paintings. As I passed by behind them, I caught a glimpse, including the damaged corners on one. Both were desirable images.

I took up a position across the room, from where I could see the dealer over the heads of his customers. I was trying to make eye contact with him. Without intending to eavesdrop, I could easily hear the discussion about the paintings.

At one point, the young lady looked to the dealer.

"Would you mind if we went out to the car and took 15 minutes to think about this?"

"No, I don't mind," the dealer said, "but I should tell you that there is someone coming from Ottawa this morning to look at the paintings."

I was shocked to hear this. Surely he could see that I was standing right there in the room. It didn't matter. Nor did our previous business history. He had a customer in front of him, and he was trying to complete that sale.

There was a long pause. I held my breath hoping the young couple would put the paintings down and delay their decision for even five minutes.

It was not to be. The young woman took a deep breath.

"We'll take them!" she said decisively.

At that point I turned on my heel and started for the door. The drive home was a long and quiet one.

Lessons learned in antiques and collecting are painful. The one I learned that morning was particularly harsh. When a dealer gives you a time, be there at that time! Someone else surely will be.

Despite the bitterness of that incident and not acquiring those two paintings, several more Lewis paintings came into my possession and I was able to more than compensate for the first one I sold as well as those two I lost to other collectors.

I have been to shows of Lewis' work in both public and private galleries and have seen many of her paintings in private collections. The Art Gallery of Nova Scotia has a permanent display of her work. The exhibition includes her actual, one-room home, which was restored, along with the contents, and moved into the gallery as part of the permanent display. Lewis decorated just about every available surface in her home with images of brightly coloured flowers, birds, and butterflies. It is a remarkable and moving experience to see the interior of this little house in which she created so many joyful paintings depicting the scenes and surroundings of her childhood.

The market for her work has surged to all-time highs and it is practically impossible for me to buy her paintings anymore on the open market. Examples of her work now sell in the $9,000 to $12,000 range, and for certain images the price can go as high as $15,000. I read about a recent sale of one her paintings that brought $22,000. It was an unusually large format and the size accounted for the record price.

While I may not be able to add more works by Lewis to our collection, I continue to search for them and still take much delight in seeing them on my travels. Any Canadian folk art collector should own or aspire to own at least one Maud Lewis painting.

The artist's world was largely confined, as an adult, to the little house just off the highway in Marshalltown in which she lived with her husband,

"Fluffy", Maud Lewis, 1963. (Acquired 1994)

Everett Lewis, and, as a young woman, to the immediate surroundings of Digby. Despite these limitations, she was able to perfectly express in her art the images of everyday life she remembered so vividly, the universal feelings of innocence, joy and humility, and the simple happiness of being that are fundamental to humans. To me, this diminutive artist from Nova Scotia who suffered and endured severe personal challenges in life is not only an iconic Canadian folk artist, but also a remarkable and extraordinary Canadian by any standard.

Germanic cupboard, Pembroke, ON, c. 1870. (Acquired 1984)

## 12

# WILNO AND THE PEMBROKE YEARS

I n antique country furniture collector circles, the name *Wilno* is legendary. It refers to the town of Wilno in Renfrew Country. Wilno and the surrounding area, including Barry's Bay, Combermere, Round Lake, and Palmer Rapids, were settled in part by Polish and German immigrants to Canada in the mid to late 1800s. There are also German settlements in West Quebec north of the Ottawa River.

Families immigrating to these areas brought with them the design styles of their home countries, which they in turn applied to the furniture and accessories they crafted on their farms. Their designs tended to be exuberant and they didn't hesitate to use vibrant colours to finish the pieces they made.

Pickers have been combing the Ottawa Valley for decades largely concentrating on the towns, villages, and farms of Renfrew County. Pickers are persistent, especially once they've discovered an important piece of country furniture. They keep notes and files on the location of objects and will return year after year until they can buy the article, or it is sold to someone else, or a family member takes it into their possession. More often than not, the picker ends up with the antique because the owner or their descendants do not value it. "Who would want that old, dirty cupboard in the shed, anyway?" is their thinking.

On repeat visits, a picker will often raise the offer price a few hundred dollars to further entice the owner to sell. It is not uncommon for a picker to return to a particular farm or house every year for 20 years or more, attempting to buy a particularly good antique. Often, more than one picker will be chasing the same piece, so the farm will receive multiple visits during the year.

One summer about 25 years ago, we rented a cottage for a week near the town of Barry's Bay. In the morning, I took the opportunity to visit the town and look for antiques. I stopped at an older frame house that was being renovated. It was a Saturday and there was no actual work being done that day but the owner was outside cleaning up debris from the interior. He gladly gave me a tour and, at one point, because the staircase had been removed, we climbed a ladder up to the second floor. There, against a wall of the house, all of the old furniture had been stored and draped with transparent plastic sheets to protect the items during the renovation.

Of all the forms of furniture made by Polish cabinetmakers in the Wilno/ Barry's Bay area, one is truly iconic – the Wilno blanket chest, or, as collectors refer to it, the *Wilno box*. Typically, the front of these pieces feature three flat panels with surrounding moulding and a high, scalloped or shaped base. But what truly sets them apart are the flowers painted on the surface of each panel. Furniture decorated with stylized forms is extremely rare, so collectors and dealers place a high value on these decorative Wilno blanket chests. Many have been found over the years, some with original paint and floral decoration intact. Many more have been found, with the original colours of the box, including the decorative flowers, covered by several layers of paint. In many cases, collectors and dealers spend hundreds or thousands of dollars having these boxes restored to their original state. This requires a restorer to meticulously remove all of the secondary layers of paint without disturbing the original layer beneath.

As we walked near to the furniture items concealed by the plastic sheets, I could see at a glance the back of a Wilno box in the middle of the other items. Although the box was turned so that its back was facing me and the front was concealed against another piece of furniture, I managed to lean over and slip my arm over the top of the box until my hand and fingers felt the front of it. I could feel the painted flowers on the front of the panel I was touching. There was no doubt that this was a decorated Wilno box, and I very much wanted it.

I stood back from the furniture and looked toward the owner.

"There's a blanket box in there. I'd be interested in buying that," I said.

"Well, I don't think that's possible," he replied.

"I'd pay a good price for it."

"Yes, I know you probably would. But the problem is that in the old days, the priest used that box as an altar and so it has a special meaning for my family."

This was the only time I had heard such an explanation for keeping an antique in the family. I simply nodded in understanding.

Although I was unable to purchase the blanket box, the family did agree to sell me a nice pine cupboard. It was in over paint and "late," probably built around 1880, but it was well constructed and in perfect condition. I was quite happy to put it in my truck. It remains with me to this day and as I pass by it, it brings back the memories of that day.

I never did hunt down another Wilno box, although I know several antique pickers who have successfully done so. But, one did eventually come into my possession. I received a telephone call from a collector who wanted to sell some items. Apparently, there wasn't enough room for his collection in his new home and he had made the decision to sell. Most of his antiques were stored in the basement and when we walked down the stairs, one of the first things I saw was a beautiful Wilno blanket box. It was polychromed with several different colours of paint and, while it did not have the flower decorations in the panels, it was still an exceptional antique. He was reluctant to sell it but after several visits and buying several other items from him, he finally accepted my offer of $1,000. It's still in our collection to this day.

When we lived in Pembroke, I toured the countryside around Wilno looking for antiques. I stopped at a small log farm where the owner, a wizened old gentleman, showed me around the property and the interior of his log house. It was fascinating to see it. All of the exposed wood in the house, every bit of it, was painted a different colour. The floor was one colour, the staircase another, the banister another, and the risers yet a fourth colour. The furniture was also painted in bright colours. Even the back of a flat-to-the-wall cupboard was painted! It was a riot of colour and the house was also as clean as a whistle.

He told me that an auction had been scheduled for the sale of all the items in the house and, since the sale bill was printed and in circulation, he couldn't sell me anything. After touring the various outbuildings, we did come upon a nine-foot bench in original red paint and a small gathering basket, which he happily sold to me because they had not been included in the sale bill. When I left, he was sitting on a cot in the corner of the main room in the log house with all those bright colours surrounding him.

Tragically, I heard some months later that the old man had fallen asleep in his barn one night and a cow had stepped on him. He died shortly after from his injuries.

I was picking with my friend Rick near Pembroke many years ago. We stopped at a farmhouse and asked about antiques that might be for sale. The young lady asked us in and took us upstairs to show us a pine armoire in one of the bedrooms. The armoire was a desirable piece of furniture and we expressed an interest in buying it there and then. If I remember correctly, the price we agreed upon was $200.

After we removed the few items that were contained inside, Rick positioned himself at one end, I lifted the other end, and we moved the big cupboard toward a back set of stairs off the hallway that descended to the kitchen. We started down the narrow staircase. I couldn't see Rick and he couldn't see me because the armoire blocked our views of each other. With much huffing, puffing and silent curses, we made our way down the stairs until, inexplicably, the armoire wedged itself between the two walls. There we were, like a ship beached on a sand bar. We couldn't go up and we couldn't go down. And there was no rising tide that was going to solve the situation for us!

"Rick," I hissed. "My end's stuck!"

"I'm stuck at this end too," he snarled from underneath the armoire.

Just then we heard another voice in the kitchen and a different woman appeared at the bottom of the stairs. I couldn't see her but could hear her loud and clear.

"What the Christ are you two doing up there!"

"Oh, hi there," Rick gasped looking over his shoulder, trying to be nonchalant while he held up his end of the armoire. "We just bought this armoire from your daughter and we're bringing it down."

"Well not today you're not!" she snorted. "Take that friggin thing back up the stairs and put it back where you found it."

"But we bought it," Rick pleaded.

"Well, consider it unbought!" the lady shouted, pointing a finger at Rick and giving him a cold stare.

We continued to struggle with the armoire. "We'd take it back up but actually we're having some trouble taking it anywhere right now 'cause it's stuck!" Rick shouted down the stairwell through gritted teeth.

By this time I managed to get high enough above the armoire to see down the staircase.

"Rick, push *and* lift from your end and maybe we can get this thing to move," I gasped, struggling mightily with my portion of the armoire.

After considerably more shoving, lifting, and pulling, the cupboard finally freed itself and we slowly moved back up the stairs with it. I cringed looking at the gouges in the walls of the staircase caused by the edges of the armoire.

"We've got it now!" Rick shouted down to the lady waiting impatiently at the bottom.

"Good for you!" she said sarcastically still leaning on the door frame at the bottom of the stairs.

After retreating back to the bedroom, we set the armoire down in its original place; both of us were hot, tired, and sweaty from the effort. We wasted little time hurrying back down the stairs, saying a hasty goodbye to the woman and her daughter. Since we hadn't actually paid for the armoire yet, there was no money to be returned. I could feel the eyes of both of them drilling into my back as we hustled out the kitchen door giggling, and walked quickly to Rick's truck parked in the driveway.

"I hope the next call goes better than that!" Rick snorted as he put the truck in gear and roared down the driveway.

"Let's hope it has wider staircases!" I replied.

I answered an ad in the *Pembroke Daily Observer* for a wood stove because I needed one for the basement of a new home we had purchased. I spoke to a gentleman who invited me to come to his house to look at the appliance, which I did one summer evening. When I arrived, he showed me the stove in a breezeway between the house and the garage. It had been a birthday present for which he had no need, so after several months had decided to sell it. I bought the stove and we chatted for a few minutes.

During the conversation, he mentioned that he had been born and raised across the river near the little village of Chichester, Quebec and still owned the family homestead. I asked about any old antiques that might be there. He replied that there were several things and he would be happy to show them to me. We made arrangements to meet there the following weekend.

The white farm house was set back nicely from the gravel concession road and while the grass was long in front, and had the look of being uninhabited, it was obvious that this 100-year-old home was well maintained. I turned in and drove up the lane to the right of the building, arriving beside a door that led into the summer kitchen. The gentleman was waiting for me on the porch. He had already begun to remove several boards that had been nailed across the opening to discourage intruders.

"I've had problems with people breaking into the place," he said, removing the final couple of boards.

"It's kind of out of the way so I can see why that would happen," I replied.

"Yeah, I drove up one day and the old pump organ was half way out the front door. I guess it got stuck and something frightened them off because they left if right there."

With the last board off, he pulled a set of keys out of his pocket, selected one, and used it to unlock the door. The old wooden door swung inward and he reached inside to turn on the light.

The room was furnished with all of the items you'd expect to see in a summer kitchen. There was a corner cupboard, a long harvest table, a bucket stand, chairs, a wood stove, and, looking a bit out of place, an impressive and early pine chest of drawers in original paint. There were empty mugs on the table. It looked as though the last people to use the place had simply got up from their places and walked out the door.

"It's looked this way for years," the man said when I commented on the furniture.

After looking around the room for a few minutes, I asked about buying the items.

"I'm tired of the break-ins," he said. "I think it's time to let it all go. If you want to buy it, make me an offer."

"OK," I said, letting a big breath slowly escape from my lips. "Let's start with the corner cupboard. I'll give you $1,000 dollars for it."

"That'll be fine," said the man.

We moved around the room and I bought everything, including the bucket bench, the harvest table, that great chest of drawers, and a folky toy "ride-em" horse. The deal completed, I brought my truck up to the door and we loaded the pieces of furniture and tied them securely. We shook hands and I drove back to Pembroke. I had just bought an exceptional load of antiques and it all started because I went to look at a wood stove!

You just never know what set of circumstances are going to lead you to the next cache of antiques.

One Sunday in 1985, Joan and I drove to the town of Fort Coulonge, about 30 minutes from Pembroke on the Quebec side of the Ottawa River. Joan had seen an advertisement for the products of a weaver whose studio was in an old house on the main street of town. It was a pleasant autumn day when we arrived and while Joan examined the various textiles for sale, I wandered to the front window and looked out. To my right and across the street was an old stone home with a For Sale sign anchored in the front lawn. A sale sign on an old house always arouses my curiosity and I made a mental note to stop at some point in the near future.

A few days later, I was travelling back to Pembroke from Ottawa and decided to go via the Quebec side of the river so I could stop at the house in Fort Coulonge that I had seen earlier in the week. Fortunately for me, the couple who owned the house was at home when I knocked on the front door.

"I stopped at your house because I noticed it was for sale and wondered if you might have any antiques to sell," I said to the man who came to the door.

"What are you looking for in particular?" he asked.

"Old pine cupboards and long tables are two of the things," I said.

"Well, there's not much left in the house but there are a couple of big pieces of furniture. One of them is a cupboard in the pantry."

"I'd really like to see them if that's possible."

"Sure. Come on in."

With that, he pushed the door open a little wider and I walked into the main hall of the gracious stone home. The homeowner took a few steps to his right and into a dining room, which was empty except for a very large Victorian walnut sideboard standing against the wall at the far end of the room. It would have once been part of an equally large dining room set with a heavy table and at least 8 to 10 chairs and likely another sideboard.

By this time, his wife had joined us in the dining room, where we chatted briefly about the huge sideboard. It's not uncommon to see a sideboard left behind when a dining room set is sold. Pieces of furniture the size of this one are simply too big to fit in contemporary homes. Turning away from the sideboard, they showed me a small hole in the floor where the wiring for a servant's bell had once been installed and which the individual sitting at the head of the table could activate by pressing down on it with his foot. Obviously, the original owner of this house was well-to-do.

With our inspection of the dining room complete, the man turned and walked toward a doorway at the far corner of the room.

Blanket chest in original paint, Wilno ON, c. 1880. (Acquired 1982)

"The other cupboard is in the pantry."

In antique hunting, the one moment I particularly enjoy is that brief time just before you see an item. I feel the adrenaline in my body start to run, and I am filled with a keen sense of anticipation, not knowing if I am about to be thrilled or disappointed.

We walked into a short hallway that led into the home's kitchen, and to the left was a doorway into a fairly large pantry. I followed the man into the pantry and he stood aside to give me full view of the opposite wall. There, standing imposingly in the small space, was a magnificent, tall pine cupboard in original paint.

After seeing hundreds of cupboards, good examples make a strong first impression. There are several key characteristics one looks for in a case piece of furniture: form, surface, workmanship, condition, and history. I knew at a glance that this cupboard was a winner in all categories. Finding an antique cupboard in original paint is rare. This one sported a dark red paint base highlighted with black paint laid over top of the red in swirls or feather-like forms. It was the maker's attempt at simulating mahogany, a wood used in formal, more expensive furniture at the time. It was common for a cabinetmaker to use pine and simulate mahogany with paint rather than use the real thing, which would presumably have been difficult to obtain in the Upper Ottawa Valley in the mid 19th century. Pine, on the other hand, was readily available.

Glass-making technology in 19th century Canada dictated the size of the panes of glass. As a rule of thumb, a cupboard with small panes of glass in the glazing is older than one with larger panes of glass. Frequently, when cupboards were meant for the dining rooms or kitchens of early Canadian homes, cabinetmakers used glazed doors with glass panes for the upper section so homeowners could display their prized pieces of china and other items. Just as frequently, however, you come across examples of cupboards that are blind, and constructed with solid doors covering both the lower and upper storage areas. This pantry cupboard was blind, and although glazed cupboards are more desirable, the other features of this cupboard offset the fact that it didn't have a glazed upper section.

The joinery of the cupboard was superbly done. All of the pine was at least an inch thick. It was "stepped back" at the waist and a set of two deep drawers had been placed just under the midline of the cupboard. There was a nicely crafted and built-up cornice adorning the top of the piece and the cabinetmaker had finished the bottom front of the cupboard with an interesting cut-out base. The cast-iron drawer handles were original and consistent with the time period when the cupboard was constructed.

Importantly, the cupboard had likely spent the last 125 years situated in the exact same spot in the pantry. It had not been moved to the basement or an out-building to be repurposed for the storage of tools and the like. When case pieces of furniture are moved to exterior buildings or basements, they often rest directly on an earthen floor. Pine may be an excellent wood for furniture but it does not tolerate moisture. Many superb Canadian pine antiques have met their end through the slow deterioration of wood rot due to damp conditions. It takes only a few years for a once-great example of country furniture to be reduced to a pile of dirty boards and mouldy dust. In this case, the pantry enclosure acted as the perfect repository for this beautiful Ottawa Valley cupboard, preserving it intact for well over a century.

I knew the moment I saw this magnificent old cupboard that I wanted to buy it. After examining the cupboard, I raised the subject of price.

"Well, we've had it appraised at $700," the man said, standing in the doorway of the pantry.

I didn't ask the name of the appraiser and I didn't care. But I said a silent "thank you" to the antique gods before turning to the owner.

"Yes, I'll pay $700 for that cupboard."

"Then it's yours," he said happily.

After leaving the house, I couldn't wait to call Joan and tell her about the latest acquisition. "Joan, you know that house in Fort Coulonge I saw last week? I stopped there today on my way home and bought a great cupboard that was in the pantry!"

"That's terrific! I've got some news too," she said.

"Oh, what's that?"

"I was at the doctor's today. I'm pregnant!"

Needless to say, the news about my antique purchase was immediately second-rate and I hurried home to see Joan and to celebrate the fact that we were going to become, later that year, a family of three!

Occasionally, since my brothers own fishing camps in the vicinity, I happen to pass through Fort Coulonge. I drive in off the highway to cruise down the main street to revisit the old stone house, the location of one of my more memorable antique finds.

At the 1987 Ashbury Antique Show with the Old Chelsea harvest table on the left and the one-board-top Lanark County harvest table on the right.

# 13

# TURNING THE TABLES

I've mentioned in previous chapters that case pieces of furniture, – predominantly cupboards – are one of my primary collecting interests. Whole collections can be built around one superb cupboard. For me, though, tables, especially long harvest tables, are almost as desirable. Like cupboards, they are large items. Some harvest tables that have been found are 10 feet in length and may come even longer although I haven't personally seen one. In collecting circles, a six-foot harvest table is the accepted minimum length. Anything less doesn't seat enough people and doesn't have the same visual impact. Having said that, I have seen and owned some impressive tables in shorter lengths.

As the name suggests, these long tables were located in summer kitchens and brought into use during the harvest, when additional seating for everyone working in the fields was required. I've owned several of these tables over the years and I am always excited to acquire a new example.

I remember one occasion when I stopped at an old farmhouse in the Gatineau Hills near the village of Venosta, not far from the family cottage. I knocked at the summer-kitchen door and an elderly man answered. I inquired about antiques, and while I spoke I could see a flat-to-the wall cupboard behind him against the far wall facing me.

"I buy old pine cupboards. Just like the one behind you." I raised my hand and pointed over his left shoulder in the direction of the far wall, where a small grey cupboard stood.

He took a quick glance in the direction of the cupboard.

"Come on in then and have a look at it."

The diminutive cupboard was nice, but I could tell at a glance that it had been made around 1900 so it was of less interest to me than an older one would have been.

Standing in the old summer kitchen I looked to my right through a doorway into his kitchen, where a long table stood with a plastic cloth covering the top and hanging down over the sides about a foot. Below the sheet, I could see the tapered legs of what was obviously an early harvest table. I asked the man about it and he invited me to take a closer look. We took a few steps into the kitchen, where I bent down and lifted the skirt of the tablecloth and confirmed that this was an excellent example of a six-foot pine harvest table. With the cloth pulled back slightly, I could also see that it boasted a two-board top, another highly desirable feature in an early table. Unfortunately the stretchers, which would have run between the legs, were missing, but I knew they could be replaced. Even with the stretchers gone and the legs repainted, you can usually see the outline of where they once joined to the table legs.

Unfortunately for me, the table, the cupboard, and several other items weren't for sale. After a few minutes of polite conversation, I left and drove back to my home in Pembroke. I did have the presence of mind, though, to leave him my business card.

Like other dealers and pickers, I have a left a trail of several hundred business cards in my path and only a very small percentage of the folks who received them ever called me back. I remember one picker telling me he was trying to buy a cupboard up in the Ottawa Valley and left his business card inside the cupboard on a shelf. When he opened the door of the cupboard there were five business cards from other pickers already inside it!

It was a surprise, then, when a few weeks later, I received a phone call from the man with the harvest table.

"Are you still interested in the cupboard and that long table you saw at my place a few weeks back," he asked?

"Yes, I am definitely still interested."

"Well, come and get them."

The following weekend I returned to his farm and together we loaded the cupboard and the harvest table into my truck.

Timing is everything in the antique business. In this case, he had discovered that part of the kitchen floor was rotten and needed to be replaced. To facilitate construction, he had to move the furniture out of the room. While he could have stored the furniture items, he opted instead to sell them to me. I was awfully glad he did.

As with most things in life, a little knowledge can be a dangerous thing. That's especially true when it comes to antiques. When you're first starting out, even after several years of handling antiques and collectibles, you routinely come across objects that you have never seen before. You may know that an item is antique and therefore has value, but what level of value in terms of dollars and cents? You can't say. This becomes problematic when you are striking a deal with the owner of an antique. You end up taking a chance or walking away without quoting a price. Or, you throw out a figure that you hope is acceptable to the seller and still allows you to resell the item at a profit. While it doesn't happen often, on several occasions I've offered too much for a piece, which of course the owner gladly accepted. I discovered after the fact that I'd paid too much, lost money on the resale, or barely recovered the purchase price.

The original highway that takes one north from Ottawa into the Gatineau Hills of Quebec is now a small secondary route (105) that follows the outline of the Gatineau River through the historic communities of Old Chelsea, Tenaga, Kirks' Ferry, Farm Point, Wakefield, and beyond. The population is a mixture of permanent and seasonal residents, many who have owned cottages along the river for generations. There are some magnificent views looking south toward the City of Hull (now called Gatineau) and Ottawa. One of my successful strategies for finding antiques is to search areas like this that are close to cities.

One day, I stopped at a small, red, one-storey house with a front porch that was quite close to the highway near Old Chelsea. I had passed by the house many times on the way to the cottage at Danford Lake and knew from the architecture that it was an early dwelling. A gravel driveway was situated about 100 feet south of the house and I pulled into it, drove the short distance up to the house, approached the back door, and knocked. A man in his 60s came to the door and I briefly explained my purpose for stopping there.

"Looking for antiques?" he said, with one hand resting on the wooden frame of the screen door. "Well, come on in and we'll take a look."

He swung open the screen door and I entered. Once inside, I knew right away that this was an interesting and very old building. The man was gracious and suggested he give me a tour.

He talked about the house and we wandered from room to room. "Actually, this building started out life as a stopping place, an old hotel, back in the horse-drawn days."

We reached the front hall and were standing in a small reception area near the front entrance. "There was a fire here years ago and it would have burned the place to the ground but they got it in time. They managed to save this ground floor and it was rebuilt as a single level." With that, he reached to his right and opened a door. Behind it was part of the original staircase that led up to the second level. The walls and stairs still showed the dark black scorch marks from the fire.

"I thought it was odd that the house only had one level," I said, staring up the staircase, which ended abruptly at the replaced ceiling. "That's a fascinating story!"

He smiled and we moved on to a front room that originally was a tavern and eating area but now served as a bedroom. Across the front hall was another large room that originally would have been used for dining but presently served as a living room. I admired several pieces of antique furniture, including a small jam cupboard in the front room and a stoneware merchant crock in the hallway placed beside a Windsor armchair still in its original colour. I knew better than to ask if they were for sale. Like all collectors, he took pride in showing me the old house and the antiques, many of which were original to this old Gatineau stopping place. We had finished the tour and were back in the kitchen at the rear of the building when I thought to ask.

"By the way, is there a basement in this place?"

"Actually, there is," he replied.

"Can you show me it?"

"Sure. Follow me."

He turned and approached a door off the kitchen, and we descended into a basement level with a low ceiling that was full of various items. He turned on an overhead light bulb. There in front of me was a long harvest table in original colour. Boxes, pails, and other paraphernalia littered the surface of the table but after clearing one section of the top, I could tell that this was a superior example. It was pine, six feet in length, a three-board top with turned legs and all in an original red colour. It was obvious that this table was original to the building and most likely had sat upstairs in the dining room. Since it had long been relegated to the basement, I thought there was a good chance I could buy it.

"I like this old harvest table. Would you think about selling it?"

"Well, I've never thought about selling it but I guess I would."

"I'd give you $100 for it," I said, standing at one end of the table.

There was a long pause while he thought about it. "It's not doing much down here. Yes, that'll be fine. But you'll have a hard time getting it out of here. We changed the staircase when we remodeled the kitchen."

I looked back up the narrow staircase. He was right. There was no way the table was going back up the way it had come down.

Pickers often face situations where large pieces of furniture won't pass through entrances and stairways. The solution is to take the piece of furniture apart, at least to a point where the sections will fit through the opening or stairway. An old picker had shown me a trick with tables.

When tables of that era were made, the ends of the apron, the vertical boards that are under the sides and the ends, were fashioned into "tenons," tongues of wood that were inserted into corresponding openings, or "mortises," in the top section of the legs. It is a method of joining pieces of wood at 90-degree angles that has been used for hundreds of years. Once in place, the cabinetmaker would drill holes through each leg and tenon, into which he would hammer wooden dowels. This secures the apron to the legs with a tight joint that will last a lifetime and longer. With the frame and legs made, all that was left to do was lay the boards lengthwise on the top and fasten them to the frame with nails driven down through the top into the edge of the apron. To reverse this process, all one had to do was drill out the wooden dowels from the tops of the legs. With a few good blows with a hammer and the legs come apart from the apron.

I assured the man that there wouldn't be a problem with extracting the table from the basement and we made arrangements for me to return the following morning. My brother Sloan agreed to come with me, and the next day saw us back at the house in Old Chelsea. We had the table apart in about ten minutes and safely stored in the back of his truck. Later that day, I delivered the table to a friend who was happy to take on the project of restoring it. When he was finished, the table looked none the worse for wear and it made a nice addition to our collection of country furniture.

On a concession road near the town of Carleton Place, Ontario, a stone home attracted my attention and I stopped. It was around lunchtime, perhaps one o' clock in the afternoon. A woman answered my knock.

"Sssssshhh!" She hissed quietly through the screen door. "My husband is taking a nap."

"Oh, sorry," I whispered, apologizing for my loud knock.

Very quietly, I whispered back through the screen door.

"I buy old antique furniture like cupboards and long tables."

She listened, and then motioned with her hand for me to step inside. We tiptoed into the kitchen where her husband was soundly asleep on a cot on the far side of the room against a wall.

"We have this table here," she whispered indicating a long table in the middle of the room.

"This is so strange," I thought. "Here I am standing in this kitchen whispering to a woman about an antique table with her husband sleeping in the same room! Can my search for antiques get any more bizarre than this?" But when you search for antiques, you learn that the circumstances around you frequently make strange twists. You simply have to be ready for anything.

I pointed at my chest then toward the table indicating I wanted to look at the table more closely. She nodded her head vigorously.

There was a tablecloth covering the table but from just a few feet away I knew I was looking at a remarkable piece of Lanark County country furniture. I only needed to confirm it. I quickly knelt down, lifted the cloth and examined the table. Her husband continued to snore lightly from his cot.

I saw that the table was a winner – at least six feet long with tapered legs and skirt still retaining an original dark red colour. Standing up, I lifted the corner of the tablecloth and quickly confirmed that it was a "scrub top." Since the surface of a kitchen table was often used for food preparation, it was left unpainted, eliminating the possibility of paint contaminating the food resting on it. The table would have been scrubbed clean after each use.

Original paint on the legs, skirt of a table, as well as a scrub top are features that are prized by collectors. Tapered legs are also preferred over turned legs because they usually indicate an earlier date of construction. Although I didn't realize it until later, this table also had a one-board top – one single piece of pine, thirty-two inches wide, had been used to construct it. One-board tops, as collectors and dealers well know, are rare as hen's teeth. I could also see from two hinge marks on one edge that the table originally had a leaf that hung off one side. The leaf would have been brought into use for larger number of family members and guests during harvest time. Even without the leaf, this was a great table.

"I really like the table," I whispered to the woman. "Can I buy it from you?" She nodded her head. "Yes, I guess so."

"How about $150," I mouthed the words so she could read my lips.

"OK," she whispered in reply.

I quietly handed her the money, which she placed behind her on a shelf. "Can I take it now?" I asked.

She nodded, then turned and walked over to her sleeping husband. I

One-board-top, drop-leaf, pine harvest table, Ottawa ON, c. 1850, as restored.

watched in astonishment as she shook him vigorously by the shoulder and said loudly.

"Honey, you have to get up now! I've just sold this man our kitchen table and you have to help him put it in the truck!"

Few if any men in his situation would have woken up, looked at his wife, and then quietly walked over and picked up the other end of the table from me, but that's exactly what he did!

Together, he yawning, we walked that superb Lanark County harvest table out of the kitchen, through the back door, into the yard, and placed it upside-down in the back of my truck. He turned and ambled back to the farmhouse where his wife stood in the doorway. I waved and so did she. As I drove out of the laneway, I was still shaking my head in disbelief.

Etched glass advertising panel for Perry Davis Pain Killer, c. 1880.

# 14

# A CASE OF EARLY ADVERTISING

M uch like fishermen and hunters, collectors and antique dealers like to talk about their conquests. Discussing the trials and tribulations of the search for coveted objects, is part of the adventure. In some cases, advanced collectors can only have a meaningful discussion on the merits of a particular class of antiques or collectibles with others who have experience and knowledge in the same field, and at that level of collecting. Typically, a purchase is only one part of an antique transaction. A good chat about recent finds, trends, and issues usually goes hand-in-hand with the sale of goods between collectors and dealers.

One weekday evening, a well-known dealer in nostalgia was at my home to buy a few things. We were in my "man cave" talking casually about happenings in the nostalgia field when a question occurred to me.

"Since we're talking about finds, is there one item of nostalgia or early advertising that you've searched for but never found?" I asked. Keep in mind that I was talking to a dealer who handles several thousand items per year and is well versed in the Canadian market for pieces of early advertising and nostalgia.

"Actually, Shaun," he said, "there is."

"And what is it?"

"They are etched coloured glass panels that were likely used as part of a display case in pharmacies around the turn of the century. There is a red panel and a blue panel, both in wooden frames. One advertises *Allan's Lung Balsam*. And the other advertises a cure for pain – *Perry Davis Painkiller*. I've been looking for those panels for years."

I was stunned!

For three years in the early 1980s we lived in Pembroke, Ontario. Pembroke is situated in the Upper Ottawa Valley and is rich in history and antiques. On the weekends I would spend time going to auctions and searching for antiques in the area, including the small towns of Eganville, Cobden, Renfrew, Douglas, and others.

One day, I had a call to visit an elderly gentleman in Pembroke to see some antiques. I arrived at his home in the early evening and I looked at a few objects he had which were not of interest to me. We wandered through a shed at the back of the house, down some steps toward a garage. We were standing in the garage chatting when he said, "I do have something here that you might like."

He walked over to the wall of the garage where the wall studs were uncovered. Reaching down into the cavity between two of the studs, he extracted a rectangular object wrapped in brown paper and brought the package over into the light of an overhead bulb. The wrapping was held in place by string but was brittle and torn. When I removed the string, the paper fell away easily from the object it was protecting.

In my hands was what appeared to be some sort of stained-glass window. I looked at it more closely. It was a dark blue pane of glass inside a wooden frame. It wasn't stained glass. It was etched. The dark blue glass had been etched into an extraordinary advertisement for a product called *Allen's Lung Balsam*. The image included a perimeter festooned with little angels. The frame around the panel showed some signs of wear but the glass panel was in perfect condition.

While I was busy examining the panel, the gentleman went back to the wall and retrieved a second package wrapped in the same brown paper.

"You've got another one?" I asked, rather incredulously.

"Yes, got two of them. Here's the other."

I handed the Allen's panel to him, took the second one from his hands, carefully untied the string, and let the paper fall away. This one was a beautiful dark red glass panel advertising a product called *Perry Davis Painkiller*. The centre of the panel depicted a small boat filled with men on a stormy sea, their lives in perilous danger. The caption at the bottom of the panel read: *Always Ready in Time of Need*. Below that phrase was another line: *Used Internally and Externally* and, finally, the words *Patented* and *Montreal* at the bottom left and right hand corners of the glass. This panel, too, was in perfect condition.

We stood under the light of a naked bulb admiring the panels.

"Where did you get them?" I asked.

"Oh, I picked them up years ago," he said. "They've been tucked inside

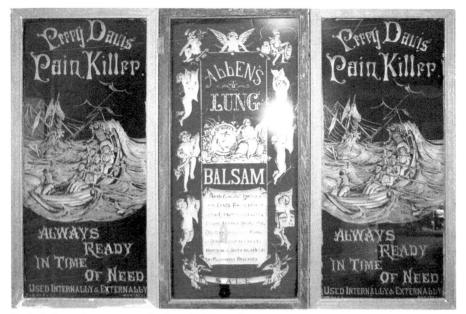

Etched glass advertising panels. (L and R) Perry Davis Pain Killer (centre) Allen's Lung Balsam.

that wall there for over 40 years."

He agreed to sell them and we struck a price of $75 dollars for the pair. I paid him. We said goodbye and I walked to the truck, where I placed the panels carefully on the seat beside me.

I had the panels at home for some time, perhaps six months or so, when my sister, Sharon, stopped by for a visit. She happened to notice the advertising panels and was taken with them. I told her that she could have them and she happily took them to her home in Toronto.

While my sister accepts the occasional gift, she often insists on paying me for the antiques that come her way through my collection. So, she paid me, as I recall, $200 for the panels. Sharon hung them in two windows in a wall beside a staircase going down to her basement. There they stayed for perhaps 10 or 15 years. Despite the many hockey bags, suitcases, and other paraphernalia that went up and down those stairs, the glass panels remained nicely intact and no damage of any kind came to them.

So, after recovering from my initial shock that day while chatting with the nostalgia dealer, I said to him: "You're not going to believe this but I know where to find a pair of those panels."

He stared back at me in amazement. "You do!" "Are they for sale?" he

The Throoptown General Store, c. 1915, could have stocked Perry Davis Pain Killer and Allen's Lung Balsam.

said, his voice rising noticeably with excitement.

"Well, I don't know. My sister in Toronto has them. I sold them to her years ago."

"Could you check with her and see if she wants to part with them?" he asked.

"I'll make the call. But first, what are you willing to pay for them?"

The dealer quoted me the impressive price of $4,000. I promised to get back to him as soon as I talked to my sister.

I talked to Sharon later that day and as soon as she heard the price the dealer was willing to pay, the etched panels were sold. Sharon generously shared the proceeds with me.

I met her in Kingston one day, retrieved the panels, and drove them to Ottawa where I delivered them into the hands of the dealer, who was ecstatic to receive them. The panels stayed in his possession for a few years until he decided to sell his entire collection of early nostalgia and advertising items at a public auction that was held exclusively for him.

I didn't attend the auction personally but heard later that the etched glass advertising panels brought the highest money of any lot in the sale – around $11,000. I think the price they fetched was as much a surprise to him as it was to everyone else in the room. I guess he felt the need to offer me some explanation as to the wide margin between what he had paid my sister for the panels and what they had brought at the auction. When I saw him at an auction a few months later he took pains to tell me that he had no idea that the etched glass would bring that kind of money. I told him not to worry about it and that he could find me a good piece of country furniture or folk art to make up for some of the discrepancy in price.

There's an old adage in antiques that, when you get a call, you have to go and see the items. You just never know what else you might find. That was true in Pembroke when I went to look at some quite ordinary antiques and made one of the finds of a lifetime – the etched glass advertising panels.

The "back" of a pine cupboard.

---- ◆●15●◆ ----

# THE BACK NEVER LIES

---- ◆●◆ ----

A veteran picker once told me that, "the back never lies." What he meant was that, when examining furniture, the backside of the piece typically reveals any deficiencies or mistakes.

In order to avoid mistakes when buying, or at least to reduce the number of mistakes one makes, the knowledgeable collector knows to examine furniture and all other antiques with careful attention. For example, one learns to look at all sides of a piece of furniture. A jagged edge on a piece of wood often means that it has been cut with a saw at a later date. The underside of arms and legs of furniture – anywhere there is exposed wood – also tells a tale. Pine should have a darker "air burned" look, and not the look of fresh wood. Subtle differences like a line or ridge of paint created where one part of the piece sat inside another tells you that a section of the piece is now missing. Design elements of the bottom portion of a piece should coincide with the top part. Be suspicious if they don't. Ask yourself questions.

With antiques, "age," "form," "surface," "condition," and "provenance" are critically important factors in gauging value. To be truly an antique, a piece's age should be at least 100 years. Form is the shape or design of the piece. Surface refers to the type of finish. Provenance is the family history of an object. Knowing the family or families who have owned an antique adds valuable information to the item's pedigree. Condition is vitally important. I have

Detail of the back of an antique pine cupboard showing cornice, air burn, and square nail construction.

Detail of the same cupboard on the right hand side, showing cornice, square nail, and air burn.

seen many remarkable antiques with so many serious condition issues that they were practically worthless. Serious collectors want pieces in original condition or with only a minimal amount of restoration and repair.

Recently, at a farm auction in Golden Lake, Ontario I discovered an interesting country wash stand. It had likely originated on that farm or nearby, and whomever made it incorporated unique ideas into its construction.

While I have seen literally hundreds of wash stands over the years, and while this one had some common characteristics, the overall form was unusual. The "cut" nails used to construct it were an indication that the stand was likely built around 1875.

The design included a shaped gallery or back splash at the rear edge; splash rails at the sides of the top, a small door, and a front, including the door, decorated with parallel beaded lines. Finally, the legs were extensions of the front and were also shaped in an interesting manner.

However, someone had recently removed the paint from this wash stand, taking it down to the raw pine. By looking at the interior, which had not been touched, I could see that the painted surface that had been removed was an interesting old green colour with traces of earlier paint peeking through it. This dark green surface should have been preserved. In its present state, all of the "surface history" of the stand had been stripped away.

Nevertheless, I bought the wash stand and spoke to the family holding the auction. They gave me the name of their German ancestors, who had originally settled the little farm where we were standing. That wash stand successfully passed four of the five tests: age, form, provenance, and condition, but failed the "surface" test. Most advanced collectors would have quickly rejected the piece, because of all those factors, surface is perhaps the most crucial. I bought it anyway, more as a memento of the day than anything else. I may have the stand painted in a period colour. It will never be as good as the original but it's preferable to the "skinned" state that it is in now.

Frequently, sections of antiques are "married." When I first started out in collecting I was quite happy on one occasion to buy what I thought was a nice antique flat-to-the-wall cupboard. As I discovered later, it was actually a chest of drawers with a glazed cupboard placed on top of it. The whole piece had the same colour of varnish so looked uniform, but it was definitely a married piece. While it was genuinely antique, it wasn't accurate, so I sold it quickly. That's what you should do: if you make a mistake, sell it, learn from it, and move on. Nothing teaches you a lesson like spending your hard earned-money on an object, only to discover that it is not "right."

Unless you find a dealer or another knowledgeable individual to advise you on the quality of an item, you're going to have to learn on your own. Don't expect other people to help you. When there's money involved, it's buyer beware. And even when you've trained your eye, you'll still make mistakes. Forged or altered antique objects frequently fool the best dealers and museum curators in the world. Learn to be dubious and fight that inner excitement upon first seeing a piece. Develop your own process of due diligence – create and use your own checklist each and every time you evaluate an antique. Examine the item, then examine it again. If you're considering a purchase from a dealer, have a discussion about the antique. Politely challenge them to outline the positive aspects of the piece. Don't be afraid to ask and discuss the pros and cons of a particular antique.

Be especially careful about "provenance". It's important, especially with higher-end pieces, to have knowledge of where they originated and, ideally, through which families they descended. If an antique has been part of a collection, it's useful to know what collector or collectors previously owned the antique you're considering buying. If a dealer or auctioneer doesn't know any details about the provenance and if you can't ascertain based on careful examination that it is "Canadian," then proceed with caution. There are many reproductions on the market and antique European country furniture has been steadily coming into the North American market for years.

On a summer day in 1983, I stopped at a little frame house in Almonte, Ontario, a small town west of Ottawa. A woman answered my knock and I asked her about old cupboards. She looked at me steadily, listening and not saying a word. At the end of my explanation, she didn't hesitate: "I have an old cupboard like that. Would you like to see it?"

"Yes, please," I replied.

I followed her as she walked briskly down the centre hall of the house through the back kitchen door and into a shed. I expected to be shown anything other than an early pine cupboard. Something in plywood wouldn't have surprised me. People routinely misinterpret descriptions of antiques. I've been in many situations where, after describing what I was looking for, I was shown something made out of orange crates in the 1950s. In this case, however, the homeowner had known exactly what I was talking about. As we entered the shed, she stood to one side.

"That's the cupboard," she said pointing to the rear of the shed.

There facing me with its back to the rear wall was a small, open dish-dresser. It was dark grey in colour, an early over paint covering the original dark red, but perfectly acceptable. The cupboard sported two nicely framed doors below the open shelving. And, separating the two sections was a pair of deep drawers. The cornice was intact except for one "return," which had been cut off – a situation that commonly occurred when the owner needed a few extra inches to make a cupboard fit properly in a particular space.

More troubling, however, was that the cupboard had been cut in two at the waist. Unfortunately, this is something one sees all too often with larger case pieces. Owners decide to move a cupboard into a basement, for example, and, realizing that it is too large to navigate down a set of stairs, they grab a saw and cut the piece in two. Many beautiful cupboards have been largely ruined by owners in this way. One of the most impressive cupboards I ever picked was from a stone house near Richmond, Ontario that had had its cornice sawn to fit through a basement bulkhead door. When cornices and returns are removed they are most often relegated to the junk pile or burned as stove wood.

In the case of the Almonte cupboard, although cut, it had been done sympathetically and the two pieces still fit nicely together.

I stood back from the cupboard, no question in my mind that I wanted it. Despite its flaws, I was certain that, overall, it was an honest and genuine piece.

"Yes, that's exactly what I look for," I said to the woman standing beside me. "I'd like to buy it."

"I don't know if I can sell it," she replied. "I'm using it for storage and I don't know where I'd put all those things that are in it."

"How about if I brought you a new shelving unit and gave you $400 for the cupboard. Would that solve your problem?"

"I think it would," she responded.

We agreed that I could return in a day or so with the replacement shelving unit. I gave her the $400 and left.

I was able to find a large used set of shelves without difficulty and returned to her home a couple of days later. I was in for another rude surprise, however, when I started to move the cupboard. Dry rot had set in to the bottom boards resting on the wooden shed floor, and at the first shove, some of the boards fell away, totally destroyed by rot. It was disappointing but, by this time I was on a mission to save this cupboard. So, despite the added damage, I took the top and the bottom sections out the back door and loaded them into the bed of my truck. It took time to find someone who would tackle the job, but eventually a dealer I knew, who was also very accomplished at restoring antique furniture, agreed to take on the project.

A few months later, the job was complete and the lit-

The Almonte open dish-dresser, c. 1840. (Acquired 1983)

tle cupboard from Almonte looked almost as good as the day it was made. The cornice "return" had been replaced, painted to match the rest of the cornice, and the bottom of the piece had been expertly restored with lumber from the same period that I had found in an old shed at my cottage.

About 10 years ago, I was picking around the south end of Ottawa along Old Highway 16 and came across a small pine cupboard in a man's garage. It was over painted in dark brown and, while it was full of many tools, paint cans, and was quite dirty, my overall impression was positive. While the cupboard was of square-nail construction, indicating a date of around 1870, the hinges on the doors were surface-mounted "tin" and of a much later date. And while that was bothersome, I assumed that they were simply "later" hinges – something that one frequently sees on antique cupboards.

Hinges speak volumes about the age of a piece of furniture.

When old cast-iron hinges broke from use, an easy solution was to mount replacement hinges on the front of the doors as opposed to trying to affix the replacements to the inside edges of the doors where hinges are typically found. While the little cupboard looked somewhat rough and abused, its owner knew it had value. He would not move off his asking price of $1,000. Somewhat reluctantly, I paid him the full amount and we loaded the cupboard into my truck.

I arrived home with the piece and stood it up in my garage where I could have a closer look. I kept returning to those replaced hinges. I asked myself, "Why are there no marks on the inside edges of the openings showing where the old hinges used to be?" There should have been. It's quite common to find a cupboard with the glazed upper doors missing. When hinges break off, it's an easier solution to simply throw the doors away rather than try to repair the hinges, especially if the cupboard is simply doing duty as a repository for old tools and paint cans.

I looked more closely at the front and the sides of the cupboard. On the sides, I could see through cracks and chips in the brown over paint that there was a beautiful dark blue, likely original paint, underneath. But I couldn't see that colour on the front of the cupboard. And then it dawned on me. Some time in the past 40 or 50 years, likely when the old doors had broken once too often, the owner decided that the best solution was to replace not only the doors but the entire face of the cupboard including the trim sections to which the doors were fastened. To facilitate matters, they simply used contemporary 1950s decorative tin hinges on the doors. A coat of brown paint over the entire cupboard matched the new front to the old sides and the job was complete.

I was disgusted with myself. I should have seen that the front had been replaced when I first examined it. My excitement about the prospect of buying the cupboard had blinded me to its flaws, and in this case, it was a major flaw. My $1,000 investment disappeared in that instant.

What is the lesson learned from this? Don't let your emotions blind you. Go through your checklist, each and every time! Make sure all the hardware matches and is consistent with the time period of the piece you're examining. Replacement hinges, for example, are acceptable if they're antique. It's com-

Hand-forged nails and green paint colour on the door help date this Lanark County chimney cupboard to c. 1840.

mon to find cast "butt" hinges that have replaced earlier styles but you should be aware of this. One inconsistency might be a clue to more significant issues. Remember, too, that over paint can conceal all kinds of repairs.

That veteran picker was certainly correct: The back never lies. And, as I discovered to my regret in the case of the little brown cupboard on Highway 16: The front can fool you, too!

Teddy Markey poses with a terrific carving by Abe Patterson of Pembroke, ON, 1991.

# 16
# Mistakes, Misfortune, and
# Missed Opportunities

My search for antiques and collectibles has not always been a success. There have been numerous disappointments, mistakes, gaffes, and faux pas along the way. I think it's only fair to share more of those experiences as well.

When you get right down to it, the difference between finding and acquiring an antique versus someone else finding it is usually one of timing, good luck, and, sometimes, money. But money alone does not win out on every occasion. Quite often the money doesn't mean anything to the owner of the object you desire. Sometimes, no amount of money will overcome sentimentality and, really, that's the way it should be. An antique passed down through the generations rightfully belongs with the next generation of the same family. But there's no guarantee that the next generation will view an item the same way their parents or grandparents did. A 19th century pine armoire that sat in the basement of a house for a hundred years or more holding preserves might be worth $4,000, but to the younger generation of that family, it's often just "that old cupboard" downstairs. That's why they will happily sell it to a picker who comes knocking and offers $100 for it.

When I was first starting out in the antiques business, I purchased a toy train set from a dealer. I should have noticed at the time that it was a reproduction, but I didn't. I drove back to his place, put the train set in front of him, complained, and asked for my money back. He agreed to refund me but added that, since I was a dealer, he shouldn't. He was right and I knew it. I didn't accept his money, took the toy train, and later sold it at a small loss.

So, early on, I learned that if you are going to call yourself a dealer, you must learn to live with your mistakes.

A fellow collector outsmarted us all at an auction to win this chest of drawers.

In the world of antique hunting, public auctions are both a curse and a blessing. There, spread out before you on the lawns and yards of a house or farm, are all the contents of a home and its outbuildings. An experienced collector or dealer can easily identify the antiques. But, you are never alone at a public auction and there is always someone else who has likely honed in on the same items as you. Early Canadian country furniture and accessories attract special attention at auctions. All of your experience, knowledge, *and* your wallet come into play when you decide to bid on an item. How much are you willing to pay? Who will bid against you? When will the item be put up for sale? Many a time I have waited practically the entire day for a certain item, only to lose it to another bidder willing to pay much more than I had estimated. I have also witnessed many epic battles at auction between two individuals who desired the same object. Rational thought often goes out the window when aggressive collectors with deep pockets spy something they want, especially if it is an object that they don't presently have in their collection. At an auction, you must be prepared for the unexpected.

Very early on in my collecting career, probably 1981 or thereabouts, Joan and I went to an auction in the village of Dacre in Renfrew County, about two hours north-west of Ottawa. The sale was held at an old farm with many interesting antiques on offer that day. What caught my eye, though, was a terrific little pine jam-cupboard in grey paint. It had a single door, hand-forged nails, pit-sawn backboards, and "rat tail" hinges. (Pit-sawn boards pre-date dimensional lumber produced with a circular saw, which leaves telltale round marks on the sawn boards.) It was an early cupboard and likely transported to the area from an older settlement somewhere else. I was excited about the jam cupboard. I decided to bid up to $150 for it. Joan and I waited until late in the afternoon when the cupboard finally came up for sale. I entered the bidding along with another individual and the price rose steadily to my limit of $150. My competitor raised the price by one more bid to $160 and foolishly I stopped at my limit. The auctioneer knocked the jam cupboard down to him for the $160 bid.

For a good portion of the drive home, I moaned and groaned about the loss of that jam cupboard and why my $150 hadn't been enough to buy it. I learned another important lesson that day. At a public auction, there is always going to be someone else who wants the item you desire. Don't set arbitrary price limits in advance. If a piece is special, then be prepared to spend a special amount of money for it. As one collector said to me recently:

"I never regretted the things I bought, only the things I didn't."

More recently, we were on our way to the cottage north of Ottawa and were taking a secondary route along the picturesque Gatineau River. Just south of the village of Wakefield we stopped at a farmhouse where the owners were holding a yard sale. I doubted there would be much in the way of antiques, as this farm must have been picked several times in the past. As I walked up the laneway, on the lawn to the left of the house, I could see a small jam cupboard in grey over paint. Even at a distance I could tell it was a genuine piece that must have been removed from the basement for the sale and was something that pickers had never seen or been able to buy. I hurried my step. I could see a piece of cardboard attached with a string to the wooden knob of the cupboard. It was fluttering in the wind. I gritted my teeth. "Please let that be a price tag and not a 'sold' tag," I muttered to myself as I rushed up to the cupboard. I reached the jam cupboard and grabbed the tag to read it. The word "SOLD" stared back at me in bold, black, handwritten letters. Frustrated, I approached the owners of the farm and discovered that the cupboard had been sold only a half hour before and the young couple who bought it had gone off to fetch a pick-up truck to move it home. The selling price was $45 dollars. It was easily an $800 piece. I was in a bad mood for the rest of the drive to the cottage.

Another time, while travelling along a secondary highway immediately south of Ottawa, I visited a farmhouse that was set well back from a road and down a lane that bridged a small creek. I parked and walked to the summer-kitchen door, where a pleasant woman met me. I explained my search for old pine furniture like cupboards.

"You mean like the one in here?" she said, pointing with her left arm to a spot inside the room. She held the door open and I took a step past the sill and looked to my right in the direction she pointed. At the end of the room was a pine corner cupboard in a dark green – as it turned out, original paint.

"Yes," I said. "That's exactly what I mean."

She invited me in to have a closer look at the cupboard. It was truly an impressive antique with glazed upper doors, flat-paneled doors below, generous returns, and a built-up cornice.

"It's from Glengarry County," she said. "I brought it here when we moved."

I admired the cupboard, which at the time was being used for storage in the unheated room. From what I could see it had no damage whatsoever except for a pane of broken glass in one of the upper doors. Without hesitation I offered her $1,000 on the spot.

"Oh, I can't sell it to you," she responded. "I promised it to friends at Church."

We talked some more about the history of the cupboard and not long after I left.

I returned to that farmhouse several times over the next year, each time increasing my offer. On my last visit, I blurted out a price of $2,000. She marched into the adjoining kitchen, picked up the phone and called her friends from the Church. I could over hear what she said.

"You'd better come and get that cupboard because the man is back again and this time he offered me $2,000 for it!"

Several months later I made my final stop there, only to discover that the cupboard was gone. But the woman was

My bid of $1,000 in 1994 wasn't enough to win this terrific hanging cupboard in original paint. (Leeds and Grenville County, ON c. 1850). The veteran dealer who won this prize knew, to be successful, you have to be the last bidder standing!

excited and wanted to show me a photo of it that her friends had taken.

"Don't show it to me," I said dejectedly. "I know what they've done. "

Despite my pleas she disappeared into the farmhouse and returned a moment later. She thrust a photo toward me and I stared at it in disgust. The new owners had had that beautiful Glengarry cupboard stripped of its original green colour and effectively ruined an excellent piece of early Ontario furniture!

Near Pembroke one day, I ventured down a long concession road to the last farm there. It was a rough and worn homestead with trucks and machinery around the yard. The man who answered wasn't particularly friendly when I explained the purpose of my visit, but he got into the spirit of things and took me across the yard to an equipment shed with open doorways. The shed housed several tractors and farm implements. We squeezed our way between the machinery to the far wall. There, lined up in a row, were four or five old pine cupboards in various shapes and sizes. One or two were particularly nice ones. He rebuffed my offers to buy them and wouldn't put a price on the items either. I went back a couple of times after that and the answer was always a polite but firm "no." I never did purchase any of them. They may still be sitting there to this day.

I received a call from a man living in Petawawa, just west of Pembroke. He said he had an Abe Patterson (1899-1969) carving that he wanted to sell. The name Patterson gets my adrenalin going like gangbusters. In woodcarving, he is in a class of his own and the stories of his carvings are legendary. Over a beer, the pickers, dealers and collectors in the Ottawa Valley are usually good for at least one story involving a Patterson carving they owned, almost owned, or tried to buy.

We discussed price over the telephone. He was asking $700 dollars. With my son, Teddy, at my side, we drove up to his home the following week and he invited us in. He had the Patterson carving sitting in the middle of his dining room table and it was impressive. The carving was a double hitch, "brag load" of logs with a team of four horses and a driver perched high on the load with the reins extended out to the horses below him. I admired the carving, which was also colourfully painted. On closer inspection, I noticed that two of the legs on the horses had been repaired but while you like to have items in perfect condition, repairs like these didn't detract from the overall impact of the piece. However, there was another, more serious, problem about to emerge related to the asking price.

The man selling the carving had earlier invited a neighbour in for a viewing of the piece who had opined that the $700 asking price was too low and should be raised to $1,000. This is a situation I've run into many times since. Friends, neighbours, and relatives are always quick to suggest that the owner is not asking enough for an antique. I have also discovered that these same individuals who suggest a higher price are never interested in paying the price themselves!

The owner broke the news to me as I was examining the carving. I was taken aback by the sudden change and he would not budge off his revised asking price. I was prepared to pay the original price but I could not coun-tenance going to $1,000. Sadly, we left that wonderful Patterson carving behind. In retrospect, I should have bought it and to this day and I regret not doing so. It has been the only Patterson carving ever offered to me in 30 years of collecting.

One other Ottawa Valley carver ranks in the same class as Patterson and, in my books, occupies an even higher place as a folk artist: Charles Vollrath (1870 - 1952) of Chalk River, Ontario. Vollrath's pieces are notable for their sensitive subjects. Take one look at a small angel he has carved and you'll immediately see what I mean. About 25 years ago, I was invited into the home of one of Mr. Vollrath's family members and shown a small china cabinet filled with his carvings. My host obviously cared deeply about his work and the pieces had pride of place in her home. I was touched by her care and concern for them and asked about buying one or two of them. She was polite but firm in telling me they would never be for sale. It was a plea-sure just to see them. One of Vollrath's angel carvings came up for at auction recently. The hammer price as I recall was in the order of $2,000.

Years ago, I answered a classified advertisement in the Ottawa paper for three Maud Lewis paintings offered for sale. The owner had decided to sell them to raise the funds necessary for her son's university tuition. The price for the three paintings was $5,000 – not a trivial amount 20 years ago!

Joan and I visited her home on a Saturday morning. We especially liked two of the paintings, but Joan didn't care for the third. We discussed buying two of the three but the owner was insistent that she would not break up the trio. After half an hour or so, we left without the paintings.

Another dealer saw the paintings after us and shrewdly offered to take them on consignment, eliminating the need to hand over the $5,000 cash. The market for Lewis paintings was quite strong back then and he had little difficulty selling two of the three in fairly short order, and he sold the third one a few months later. I wish I'd been as smart as he was in offering the consignment option.

I received a telephone call to visit a woman in the west end of Ottawa to look at some paintings. I wrote down the address and a day or so later called at the apartment building where she lived. She invited me in and introduced me to her son, who was visiting her and helping her make deci-sions about the paintings. It became apparent immediately that this was no ordinary collection of paintings. There, hanging on the walls of this modest apartment, were works by members of the Group of Seven, including a large

In 2004, I was the successful bidder on this exceptional pine storage cupboard. It took $3,000 to win it, which proves you often have to pay a premium to acquire an excellent antique.

canvas by A. Y. Jackson. In adjoining rooms, paintings by lesser-known but still highly collected artists were stacked, unframed, against the walls.

While I admired the paintings that day, I knew right away that I was out of my league and that the woman and her son should be talking to an expert in Canadian art. While I certainly recognized the artists represented in the collection and appreciated that these paintings were worth many thousands of dollars, I was not an expert in that field and these paintings for the most part were far beyond my expertise and my financial resources. I might have been able to buy some of the lesser works or strike some other arrangement, but the sheer scope and volume of the collection was, at the time, too intimidating. I made some polite excuse and left. I don't know what happened to that impressive collection but I am sure that some auctioneer or dealer was only too happy to assist with its dispersal.

One Saturday morning in Pembroke, I stopped at a man's house. If I remember correctly, he was having a yard sale. He had a large double garage at the end of his laneway behind the house. In the right-hand side of the garage he kept a 1961 Cadillac Biarritz convertible. It was mauve in colour with a white leather interior. I believe he said the car was 21 feet in length. It fit into the garage with only a few inches to spare. Among the articles in the left side of the garage, there was an over painted cupboard that had reasonably good but not superior form. I expressed interest in the cupboard and we agreed on a price.

Then I noticed that beside the cupboard was a large wooden barrel filled with items wrapped in paper. I asked about the contents and he proceeded to unwrap one or two of the packages. As it turned out the barrel contained over 100 pieces of transfer-ware china with various scenes of old Quebec City on them. I recognized them immediately because this china is quite rare and sought after by collectors. I wanted to buy the lot and I returned several times after that, but was always unsuccessful. Then one day I attended an antique show at the Ottawa convention centre. As I rounded one of the aisles, there set up in a booth was the gentleman from Pembroke with a table upon which sat all of that fabulous transfer-ware china. I stopped to talk to him and expressed my surprise at him being there. I never saw him again at an antique show or otherwise. I presume he successfully sold that beautiful china.

In Perth, Ontario, a gentleman took me on a personal tour of an impressive Georgian-style stone home. Room after room, upstairs and down, we walked through the entire house. There wasn't a single antique of merit in the place. The carriage sheds next to the house were almost as unproductive, until he unearthed three antique broadsheets – posters from the mid 1800s. One advertised a local mill available to grind wheat into flour. Another one advertised a stud horse, showing a large image of the animal, available for breeding purposes. The man had found them in the walls of the carriage shed during a renovation. I bought all three for $90 and was satisfied to have them, but it didn't entirely quell the disappointment of finding absolutely nothing in such a gorgeous stone home.

If I had a nickel for every room, attic, shed, or barn that turned out to be empty rather than full or had nothing in it worth buying, I could take Joan on a cruise! I well remember when the owner of an old Victorian home spent half an hour, at my repeated suggestion, slowly removing the nails from a door to a rear shed that had been nailed shut for 50 years. It had been so long that even he couldn't remember what was in the building. When the door finally creaked open and I had a glimpse of the interior, it was completely empty.

On occasions, I have come across houses and farms that appeared to be abandoned with doors unlocked, and yet with all kinds of antiques still inside. With one exception, when Joan and I helped ourselves to a harvest table whose legs had been pretty much eaten away by porcupines, I have generally avoided seemingly abandoned houses in the countryside. If an unoccupied house catches your attention, make the effort to find the owner. That extra bit of research can pay off handsomely and you'll avoid any issues with trespassing.

Part of the reason I started picking was to find antiques in their original settings, where they were actually constructed. If I found a pine bucket bench or and old flat-to-the-wall cupboard in a barn or a summer kitchen on a farm in the Ottawa Valley and the people who owned it could tell me how long it had been there and perhaps who made it, I could be fairly certain that the piece was genuine. Besides, there is nothing like the feeling of excitement one gets from being the first to find an important item and bring it out into the open.

At an auction, a flea market, or antique shows, there are no guarantees. Some dealers are willing to vouch for the authenticity of what they sell. Some will even buy a piece back from you, albeit at a reduced rate. But many dealers simply stock their shops with items they think, based on experience, will sell. Simply because a particular type of object sells well, doesn't mean it is genuine or antique.

People make buying decisions based on their personal taste and impressions. The impulse buy is as common in the antiques trade as it is anywhere else. Antique dealers, like all merchants, are responding to market trends and influences. But a market trend does not always align with quality. If an individual wants to buy a harvest table that simply looks old because it was made today from old barn board, that's their prerogative. If they want a cupboard and it happens to be European and not Canadian, there are plenty of dealers who will sell them one.

At an antique show or any other place of sale, the only assurance you have, besides your own knowledge and experience, is if the dealer is willing to give you a written guarantee of an item's authenticity. Reputable dealers will do that and tell you everything they know about the background of a piece.

If you are genuinely interested in antiques, you must fight your way through all of the trendy merchandise that clutters the current market. Focus on your area of collecting and identify what the best of that market is. Study and learn why it is the best; visit the shops and the dealers who handle that type of item and talk to them. You'll learn more in 15 minutes from talking to a reputable dealer than you will through long conversations at the lower end of the market. Fortunately, high-end dealers are more than willing to talk about their offerings.

Start small. Research and buy an item of reasonable quality and learn from that experience. Restrain yourself from purchasing a major item until you've built your experience, your knowledge, and your confidence. When it is time to add a cornerstone piece to your collection, you'll enjoy it that much more knowing you've prepared well for the acquisition. Early on, you'll have to decide if you are building a serious collection or simply acquiring a few objects for interest's sake. Although I have handled hundreds of pieces and redecorated my house many times over, if I was to start over again I would spend the same amount or more, but on far fewer items.

Over the past 30 years, I have purchased many antiques and collectables at flea markets, antique malls, group shops, and similar venues. These markets are tempting to all collectors but pose both an opportunity and a challenge.

Antique markets are typically large and have many vendors of different types and quality. While diversity means the selection is greater, it also heightens the risk that the selection will include inferior items, reproductions, fakes, and forgeries. Standards are often loose or non-existent, and difficult or impossible to enforce. The vendors' experience in the business may vary widely, from seasoned veteran to complete beginner and everything in between.

Typically, managers of antique and flea markets lack specific antique collecting experience. Their expertise is usually more logistics and administration. Owners and operators of large markets don't care as much about the products offered as they do about renting out the stalls each week. There are some exceptions. For example, the weekly *St. Lawrence Market* in Toronto has a picker in charge of its operations.

At public markets, the collector must be alert and have a mental "due diligence" checklist at the ready. To buy antiques successfully, the collector must know more, or at least as much, about a particular type of item as does the vendor. If you know less than the vendor, then you are at a disadvantage.

Compare that to the scenario of an advanced collector or dealer, when he visits a public market. The advanced collector does know as much, and often much more, about a specific area of collecting than the average weekend vendor at a public market. That gives him a distinct advantage.

It's easy to visit any antique market and find items priced at fair market value. The advanced collector attends the market on the chance of finding items of interest that are priced *below* fair market value. We've all read stories in the newspapers about fabulous antiques and art objects found at flea markets for a few dollars that turn out to be worth thousands and occasionally millions of dollars. Finding and buying an antique at a market for next to nothing when it's worth thousands is a rare occurrence. Buying an item for $10 that's worth $300 or $400 occurs frequently.

Last year, I found a terrific folk-art painting at a large outdoor flea market. I paid a few dollars for it and sold it for $325. I probably could have sold it for more. Once you've done this, you are motivated to try it again and again.

I've also been on the other end of this type of transaction. In the early days of my collecting and dealing career, I have been the one that sold an item at far less than its retail value.

I remember stopping at an old stone house near the town of Richmond, Ontario. A middle-aged couple was there that day and we chatted about antiques. As it turned out, they were from Windsor, Ontario but planning to retire to the farm. In the meantime, their son was staying there while attending college in Ottawa. I asked about old cupboards and they took me into a shed at the rear of the house. There, up against a wall, was the base of a large flat-to-the-wall cupboard.

What set this cupboard apart from most was its design and construction. Both doors and the sides of the cupboard had raised panels within frames,

twelve in
all: four on
each door and
two on each side
of the cupboard base
– a very desirable feature
in early Canadian furniture.
I examined the cupboard more
closely and noted that it had orig-

Germanic table of unusual and rare form. Shown here in "as found" condition shortly after I picked it near Pembroke, ON, in 1985.

inal red paint and was made of thick pine. The nails and hinges indicated an early date of construction, likely around 1840. I was excited but had to caution myself because this was only half of the cupboard. I knew it originally had an upper section.

"This is a good cupboard. But it would have had an upper section. Would that still be around?" I asked the couple behind me.

The woman replied, "I don't know. We've never been asked that before. It could be here."

"Do you think we could have a look?"

"Yes. Where would you like to begin?"

"I saw bulk-head doors for the basement at the side of the house. Could we look there?"

"Let's do that," she replied.

We made our way around the west side of the house to the bulkhead doors, which opened without difficulty. A short flight of four or five stairs led into a dark basement with a low ceiling, but high enough that we could walk around with our shoulders hunched.

It didn't take long to make the discovery. Against the far wall of the basement sat the upper section of the cupboard. Behind its original glazed doors, preserve jars and other containers sat on several shelves. I suspected that it had been in the basement for many years and used for extra storage. Whomever had moved this top section of the cupboard into the basement had realized that it was too tall and would not fit underneath the joists. Their solution, as is often the case, was to saw off the cornice of the cupboard, thereby reducing the height by some six inches and allowing it to stand upright. It was upsetting that the cornice was missing. I made a half-hearted attempt to find it nearby but I knew it was long gone. While the missing cornice and the damage created from removing it was serious, I was certain it could be restored. Cornices are often missing from case pieces of furniture.

After a few minutes in the cellar, we made our way back up the steps and outside. As it turned out, the homeowners were planning to install a new furnace, the price of which was estimated at $2,300. When I heard that, I knew the price of the cupboard.

"Then I'll give you $2,300 for it," I said without hesitation.

"You can have it," the lady replied.

Because it was such a large cupboard, I called my brother, Sloan, to come with his truck and help me. While we waited for him to arrive, I bought several more small antique items from the back shed and the kitchen. About 45 minutes later we loaded the two pieces of the big, red flat-to-the-wall cupboard into the back of Sloan's truck and returned to Ottawa where we unloaded it into my garage. Even without the cornice, I couldn't set the top of the cupboard onto the base. It was well over eight feet in height.

Later that evening, the first doubts about the cupboard began to creep into my mind. Was it too tall? Did I pay too much for it? What was the restoration going to cost? There were no panels on the top section so did that mean the top wasn't correct? On and on went the questions in my mind until finally, I called a dealer and asked him to come look at the piece. He showed up at my home a few days later and quietly looked at the cupboard.

He quickly agreed to my price of $2,850 and we loaded the cupboard into the trailer behind his van. I felt a sense of relief when he drove away, but at the same time, I wondered if I had acted in haste. Looking back on it now some 12 years later, it's clear to me that the piece was exceptional and a far better cupboard than I had first realized. Of course, that's all hindsight. At the time, I had handled perhaps 50 cupboards in total. The dealer to whom I sold this one had bought and sold hundreds if not thousands of antique pine cupboards.

I once found a set of drawers that was likely used in a general store for the storage of various items. Made of butternut, it had four rows of small drawers, sixteen in all, which graduated in size top to bottom, from shallow to deeper. The piece was sizeable, roughly five feet wide and five feet high. I had found it in a shop on the Quebec side of the Ottawa River. It was over painted but I was confident that, once refinished, the chest would be a very good one. The dealer was happy to sell it to me for $160. Later that autumn, refinishing complete (I was doing the work myself back then), I took the piece with me to a show in Ottawa and set it up in my booth. I put a price on it of $1,100. A veteran dealer came by early in the show. He took one look at the chest, turned to me and said, "Shaun. Put a sold sticker on that piece."

Why did he act so quickly? He knew that graduated chests like that one are rare; especially larger ones that are intact, and all of their drawers and turned knobs in place. And, it was a local piece. While I had refinished it, I didn't over do it and much of the original red colour was still there. That was 25 years ago. To this day, I've seen perhaps two or three more examples of this type of chest and the one I owned was as good or better than any of them.

That's the reason savvy dealers and collectors show up at public markets early, often at 7:00 A.M. or as soon as they are allowed into the building or onto the site. They know that, to find under-valued or special items for their collections, they have to be there at the beginning of the event. Many antique show promoters have recognized this fact and charge a higher admission fee to enter the event as dealers are setting up their booths. For a determined collector, the higher admission fee is inconsequential compared to the advantage it gives them of viewing the antiques on offer before others arrive.

As you approach the top of the market in any area of antiques and art, the number of dealers who operate at that level are fewer in number. Prices for objects are higher because the quality of the items is greater, but the number of available customers is decidedly smaller. The majority of antique dealers do business at the middle or lower end of the chain. There simply isn't as much risk in buying less expensive items to resell than there is at the high-end of the market.

So, imagine a high-end dealer or collector wandering through a public market or a typical weekend antique show. Does that expert's knowledge level and buying power give them an advantage over the majority of customers and dealers at that show? It most certainly does. Experienced dealers often make a practice of picking antique shows and shops, buying items they know are underpriced, then moving up-market to customers who are willing to pay a correspondingly higher price. Some collectors will buy from a particular dealer only, one who has a reputation for handling a certain quality of merchandise. In that dealers' possession, the antique enjoys an enhanced level of credibility. Higher quality items find their way to higher-end dealers.

When we buy contemporary objects, we base our buying decisions on factors such as price, form, colour, functionality, availability, etc. If you are buying an item and functionality is the primary consideration, its value and authenticity as an "antique" is secondary, which is fine as long as you, the buyer, know in your own mind that function is the key factor and not the antique merits of the particular object. That's why reproduction harvest tables made from old lumber, for example, sell so readily. The buyers want the look of an antique but don't care if the piece actually is an antique. It's also why imported antiques sell well in the North American market. The buyer who wants an antique cupboard isn't necessarily concerned about its pedigree. One from Eastern Europe, recently imported here, will fit the bill nicely. Many dealers are willing to supply that demand.

If an item is inexpensive it reduces the impact of price as a factor in the buying decision. If, however, the antique merits of a piece are important, that's a different story. When price becomes a factor, the buying decision becomes much more complex.

New collectors are wise to focus on particular types of antiques. It helps target the search, and learning about a specific category of antique prepares and educates the new collector *before* buying.

Buying an antique, regardless of where you find it, always has challenges, but if you plan and think carefully about what you are trying to accomplish in terms of a collection, you can start out on a solid footing and eliminate much of the self-doubt and mistakes that often accompany the early days of collecting.

Buying from a reputable dealer's shop as opposed to the public market setting doesn't relieve a collector of the need for due diligence, such as comparisons with similar antiques in other shops, research on the Internet, or obtaining a second opinion from a fellow collector. However, buying from a reputable dealer who specializes in the particular type of antique you wish to buy will narrow your search, focus your selection on presumably higher-quality items, and can provide some guarantee of authenticity and a return policy. Reputable dealers believe in what they are selling and will most often agree to take back a piece if there is a legitimate problem with it.

So, accept the fact that you will make mistakes along the way. Try to minimize them by being prepared. Celebrate your successful finds and enjoy your antique discoveries. As you progress in your learning and understanding of antiques, be prepared to share your knowledge with others.

A full load of antiques, 1985.

# 17

## PICKING PARTICULARS

D ue to the popularity of television shows devoted to the topic, "picking" has recently come into the public spotlight. *American Pickers* is a popular television show on the History Channel in the U.S. with several million viewers per episode. *Canadian Pickers*, the Canadian version of the original, also proved to be popular in this country until its demise after four seasons. *The Antiques Road Show* continues to be a top-rated program on public television in the U.S. (Apparently, the concept of that show isn't good enough for television in this country – the Canadian version was not renewed after a run of a few seasons, and ended several years ago. The original British series upon which both North American versions were based has been running for over 35 years in the U.K.)

In a typical episode of one of the shows, the hosts arrive at a pre-determined location, often a dealer's shop and sometimes a private home, to which they've been invited to view and possibly buy antiques. A search through the antiques and collectables ensues and the pickers make their finds, purchase them, and move on to the next stop. This brand of picking bears little resemblance to antique picking in the real world. The contrast between the two is understandably lost on the viewing public, who can't know the difference.

A pre-arranged visit to someone's home after they have contacted you is not picking. In the business, that's known as a "house call."

Visiting an antique dealer's shop and buying items is also *not* picking. That's simply buying from another dealer. Some might argue that buying from a dealer is "shop picking," and to some extent that's true, but it's a far cry from true house and farm picking.

Attending an antique show – be it one held indoors or in a field – and buying antiques from the participating dealers is *not* picking.

Unloading antiques in Ottawa ON, 1985.

While I'm on the topic, badgering the bejesus out of a dealer to get the price down as far as possible on an item, as is often depicted on the television shows, is definitely *not* picking. That's known as "grinding" and is most unpopular with dealers. The majority of dealers are receptive to a reasonable offer on their items but when someone grinds away at you, over and over, then comes back one last time to grace with you with their "final offer," it's downright maddening. Dealers dig in their heels and, at a certain point, would rather not sell the item at all than to sell it to someone who tries the full-on bargain-basement approach.

These distinctions around what is and is not picking are important to the professionals in the business. So, then what is picking?

The purest form of picking is going door-to-door, unannounced and uninvited, and inquiring about antiques that might be for sale. About the only similarity between this activity and the one depicted on the television shows is that there are antiques involved.

When I say door-to-door, I mean *every* door. A professional picker leaves no stone unturned. He or she will stop at every farm or every house on a particular road or street. The law of averages applies just as well in antique picking as anywhere else. The more places you stop, the better your odds of finding antiques. While the television shows don't specifically mention it, most professional pickers work every day.

I once met and chatted with a picker in Atlantic Canada. He happened to be staying at a motel near ours and I noticed his truck when he pulled into the parking lot. It was pretty hard to miss, since it was piled high with antique furniture. During our conversation, he told me his practice was to pick every day for a month. He then took the next month off. (After picking for 30 days straight, I'd be ready for a long stay in a rest home!) He worked all week, and when the truck was full, he'd take the load to an auction where all of it was sold to dealers. When the auction was over, it was back on the road to re-fill the truck.

He said that this routine, one month on and one month off, continued all year except for the month of March, when he went to Florida for a well-earned winter vacation. Besides, picking in the winter has its own challenges. It's often impossible to get a barn door open when there's several feet of snow and ice blocking your way. "Come back in the spring" has been heard by every picker who got behind the steering wheel of a half-ton truck.

The practice, as depicted on television, of buying one or two items and then moving on to the next stop is ridiculous. I'm sure I'm not the only experienced viewer who yells at the television: "Hey, what about the pine harvest table you just walked by!" The professional picker buys anything and everything that has "age." They are not selective in terms of category. The professional picker buys it all: furniture, lighting, architectural pieces, toys, signs, glass, china, paintings, prints, clocks, watches, jewelry, stoneware, musical instruments, boats, canoes, fishing tackle, and so on. As long as the item has some antique value and can be bought at the right price, the object goes into the truck. The professional picker knows there is a market for everything! The professional picker may also stop at dozens of houses and farms – and not buy a thing. If you have any issues with rejection, believe me, you won't want to try picking antiques for a living.

If a professional picker sees an object but is unable to buy it, a note is taken and the picker will return the next year and the year after. I know some pickers who have chased desirable items for as long as 20 years before circumstances finally allowed them to make the purchase. I also know some pickers who have chased items for 20 years and lost them simply because they took a year off and didn't stop at the farmhouse. One veteran picker told me that a cupboard he had been trying to buy for years had no less than five business cards in it from various pickers and dealers. When a piece isn't for sale, the best you can do is leave a business card and hope one day to get a call from the owner. They rarely do call back.

Some pickers travel with detailed maps showing all of the rural concession roads in a particular area. They mark the map showing where they've seen quality antiques and weren't able to buy them. If you've been in a hundred barns, sheds, and basements, it can be a challenge to remember which piece you saw in which location. A map with detailed notes is a practical solution to that problem.

The best pickers I know are quiet, unassuming individuals who can earn the trust of a stranger in a matter of seconds. You could pass them on the street and never notice them. But, behind those quiet exteriors are individuals with almost encyclopedic knowledge of antiques and collectables. You could drop them in a house full of antiques and collectables and in 10 minutes they could give you a detailed assessment of the quality, quantity *and* commercial value of all the antiques in the entire place. And, unless an item is hidden under the floorboards in the attic or a similar hiding place, they won't miss a thing.

At times, picking can be brutally unfair to those who possess the antiques. Few individuals can resist buying an antique object for a low price if the owner accepts the offer. A picker wants to get the item at the lowest acceptable price or something close to it. The lower the buying price, the larger the profit margin will be for everyone in the chain of dealers who sells the piece thereafter. When buying antiques as a picker, the challenge is to be fair about the price paid while at the same time not being aggressive and paying too much. Often, it's a fine line.

A picker told me once that people *always* have a price in mind for an item. They may insist that they don't, but nine times out of 10 they do. The challenge is to get the owner to reveal that number. Once they do, it makes the buying much easier.

Pickers know that others are on the hunt and right behind them. I recall picking a house in Brockville where an elderly gentleman kindly invited me in to look around at his possessions. He also added that I was the third picker to stop at his house that *week*! Needless to say, there wasn't a thing left to buy.

If they can't buy an antique from the owner, some pickers will intentionally hurt the prospects of the next picker by making a very high offer on a particular item. While the large amount of money offered won't buy the antique, it makes the next picker, who offers a fraction of that amount, look silly by comparison and strengthens the reputation of the picker who made the generous offer.

The first cupboard I picked. Embarrassingly, the top portion is upside down.

Professional pickers are well organized. Some travel in pairs with two vehicles. Their routine is to stay in a local motel for a week and pick the rural areas. They leave a large cube van at the motel, into which they place all of the items they buy during the week. At the end of the work week the cube van is hopefully full and they leave to take their merchandise to a dealers' auction. The following week they start the process over again in a different location.

Another model of dispersing finds is to hold a private dealers' "pick." The picker returns to home or his place of business with a load of freshly picked antiques, then makes a call to the area dealers with whom they regularly do business, inviting them all to the "pick", where the items are priced and spread out for examination. Each participant selects a number and "number one" gets to choose first and purchase the item of his choice from the picker. This process continues until each dealer has selected an item. The process is then repeated until all the items have been sold. This method of dispersal is rare these days.

A variation on this model is to invite high-net-worth individuals to attend the sale of a private collection. The same process is followed, albeit at usually much higher prices, until all of the items are sold. I believe this was the process that was used in New York City many years ago to disperse at least a portion of the Gertrude Stein collection of French impressionist and post impressionist paintings. It was also used for the dispersal of a well-known collection of Canadiana in 1999, which featured many prized pieces of "Wilno" Polish antique furniture.

This mode of dispersal also avoids the public auction method, which can at times be susceptible to "pool" bidding. A pool refers to buyers who agree before the auction that they will purchase certain items as a group. The action undermines the usual competition found at auctions, and as a result, the items sell for less than they would under normal circumstances. After the event, the pool of buyers holds another private auction of the items they purchased. The winning bidder pays the original amount required to obtain the item at the auction plus the additional amount generated by the second private auction. The total is then divided among the members of the pool. However, in the eyes of the law, pool bidding at auction is illegal and some jurisdictions have specific legislation prohibiting the practice.

Dealers typically rely on auctions for a significant percentage of their stock. At a sale, some dealers try to protect their turf by bidding steadily against others for the type of merchandise in which they specialize. It's their attempt to discourage collectors and members of the public from buying at the auction rather than buying the item in their shop.

I remember at one auction many years ago, there was a tiger-maple sewing stand that caught my eye. After a few hours, the stand came up for sale and the bidding started. I happened to be standing with a well-known dealer. After some spirited bidding from a number of people including myself, the auctioneer was about to sell the item to me for my bid of $350 when the dealer turned in my direction and whispered to me. "Sorry to do this but I have to." With that he raised his hand and made the next bid. I countered with another bid and we continued on until a price of $700 was reached. At that point I guess he figured he'd made me pay enough and dropped out of the bidding. The auctioneer knocked the stand down to me for the $700. There was a buyer's premium of 10% on top of the hammer price as well. I later sold the sewing stand for $1,100, but at the time I thought I had paid too much.

Over the years, I adopted a personal rule for auctions. When I saw an item of interest, I would quickly come up with a figure in my mind that I would be happy to pay for it. Then, I *tripled* that estimate as the likely outcome of the bidding. My thinking was that if I acquired the item in the low range of the estimate it was a bargain. If I had to pay at the high end of the estimate, I was paying closer to fair market value.

For generations, thousands of superb Canadian country antiques have been taken across the border and sold in the U.S. This was especially true in years when there was a huge gap in the exchange rate between the Canadian and U.S. dollar. At the time, with a 25 to 30% difference in the exchange rate, there was a tremendous incentive to sell Canadian antiques into the U.S. It's true, too, that many Canadian antiques become "American" antiques once they cross the border. One of the nicest cupboards I ever owned found a new home in the U.S. after I sold it to a Canadian dealer.

As a picker, you are often confronted by antiques that you've never seen before, and for which you have little or no idea of market value. But, you are there to buy, so you are likely going to make an offer. The natural tendency is to keep the offer low and, hence, keep the risk to you low. I'll be the first to admit that, on several occasions, I could have and should have paid more for certain items. When you buy an object for little money, it essentially reduces your risk to almost nothing and that's difficult to resist. On the other side of the equation, on many occasions I paid too much for antiques and in the end lost money. Hopefully, in the grand scheme of things, everything has balanced out.

Searching for antiques at the source – in a dusty attic, a dark basement, an old barn – is a unique experience. For me at least, the sense of discovery and the emotional high associated with an important find is more intense than searching the inventory of an antique dealer's shop or warehouse. So, I'll continue to "pick," albeit far less frequently now. I know the antique treasures won't be as easy to come by as they once were, but still the thrill of the hunt is just as intense and just as much fun. Sometimes it isn't about the money and the profit.

LaChute Flea Market, Lachute QC, 2013.

# LaChute

In the universe of antiques in Ontario and Quebec, one venue has no rival – the *LaChute Flea Market*. LaChute, as everyone refers to it, has been operating continuously for over 35 years. It is a sprawling complex of buildings, barns, garages, and open spaces that attracts dealers of all types of products, including antiques.

The LaChute market is legendary among collectors and dealers and I had often heard stories about the fabulous finds and great deals made there. Tuesday is the day for antiques at LaChute. At peak season in the summer, pickers, dealers, and collectors from far and wide arrive in the early morning hours before dawn to ensure they obtain one of the outdoor spots from which to sell. The buyers are there just as early! Although I had heard many stories, I had never visited the iconic market, situated about 45 minutes west of Montreal.

Two years ago, I decided the time had come to "do" LaChute. I gathered up a truckload of antiques and collectables and made plans for to be there the following week. Once again, I enlisted the help of my brother, Scott, who also had several antiques that he had decided to sell. Everything went into the truck and off we went to LaChute. We arrived there when it was still dark, around 4:30 in the morning, and found a vendor spot opposite one of the parallel interior roadways.

"This spot looks as good as any, Scotty," I said, maneuvering the vehicle so it was parallel to the lane and slightly underneath the overhanging branches of a line of spruce trees separating the rows of vendors.

"Yeah, it'll do," Scott replied. "Cripes, sure is dark, though."

I had barely put the transmission into park when beams of flashlights cut through the rear windows of the vehicle and illuminated the interior. We emerged into the darkness. Already, there were a dozen dealers and

After the early morning rush of dealers, my brother, Scott, stands in our nearly empty vending space at the Lachute Market.

collectors surrounding the truck, shining their flashlights and peering into the window to view the antiques we had on board.

A bright light about a hundred feet down the lane to my right caught my eye as I stepped out of the truck. I could tell at a glance it was a television camera and its accompanying light. The cast and crew of the *Canadian Pickers* television show were shooting a segment for the upcoming season. Too bad they were down the row past our booth, because the real action was right in front of me!

I turned my attention back to our situation, which was becoming intense as more dealers and collectors descended on us. "Have any advertising items?" one individual asked.

"We might," I replied. "Just give us a minute to get organized."

"How about lighting fixtures?" another yelled.

"Anything early in pine?" another voice called out.

"What about stoneware?

"I buy old toys," said another collector.

As we opened the tailgate of the truck, the questions kept coming in rapid-fire succession. At LaChute the dealers and collectors are polite but enthusiastically aggressive. They know that to stand back is to possibly lose out on an important piece. They're especially keen when they see a new vendor driving onto the field, one that may have good items available at equally good prices.

"Can I help you unload?" a dealer asked, standing at the back of the truck. Scott had got the ropes untied and was handing down furniture to people below him on the grass.

"Sure," I replied. "Put this on the table my brother just set up."

"I'd like to see what's in that box. Mind if I open it?"

"I guess not," I replied. "But be careful."

I grabbed an Ottawa stoneware merchant crock from behind one of the seats in the truck and put it down on our table. A hand came out of the crowd, pressed against the table, and grasped the edge of the crock. "Hey Ken, come here and look at this!" the owner of the hand shouted to his left into the darkness. It was obvious he was staking claim to the crock until his friend appeared. He was joined a moment later by a dealer who took over from him.

"How much do you want for the Ottawa crock?" Ken asked me.

"$350," I said, without missing a beat.

"Would you take $300?" he asked.

"Yes," I said just as quickly.

The money changed hands. The crock was gone and I turned to face more dealers and collectors to hear their offers on the antiques they were "helping" us to unload from the truck.

The buying frenzy continued for half an hour until gradually the early-bird crowd of dealers and collectors around us thinned out to a handful of diehards who were still examining items or dickering on prices with

A recent folk art find from the LaChute Market. Painted wood panel by B. Boisjoly, 2002.

Painted wood panel by B. Boisjoly, 2002.

Scott and me. For example, Scott had brought a maroon-coloured radio by the maker *FADA* with beige-coloured knobs. While one of the knobs was missing, it was still a much-sought-after model and Scott and a collector were haggling to find a mutually agreeable price.

In the area immediately next to us, another dealer who had arrived earlier, and whose merchandise had not caused the same type of interest, watched from a distance. When the last dealer left the side of our truck after buying Scott's collection of Bee Hive hockey photographs from the 1950s, the dealer walked over to me.

"Holy Jesus!" he said to me. "What were you guys selling?"

"Just good antiques and collectables," I replied while cleaning up the wrapping paper and empty cardboard boxes that were strewn around the side of the truck. And it was true. Since it was our first time at the LaChute market, we planned on bringing quality items, objects that we knew were highly collectable. We expected a demand, but, admittedly, we weren't prepared for the melee that ensued.

Later that season at LaChute, one dealer who saw an antique table strapped to the top of my truck ran along side the vehicle and rapped his knuckles on the body while he yelled: "How much for the sawbuck table?"

By 1:00 P.M. some of the vendors start to pack up and leave the market. They know that if they haven't sold their items by then it is un- likely there will be any more sales, or at best only a few.

A veteran dealer told me later that the way to avoid the rush we experienced was to park

A third painted wood panel by B. Boisjoly, 2002.

your vehicle, lock it, and walk away. That way, he said, you can browse the other vendors' merchandise at the market.

"When you're good and ready, like in an hour, come back and open your vehicle. The dealers and collectors will still be there, and still keen."

I tried his approach the next occasion and it worked reasonably well, although one or two dealers followed me through the crowd asking about items they could see in my truck. It's nice to be wanted!

Another long-time dealer told me that, in its heyday 15 to 20 years ago, the LaChute Market was the epicenter of antiques in Quebec. Pickers came from all over the province and brought huge loads of often spectacular an- tique pine furniture and accessories to sell.

The LaChute Market may not be today what it was back then, but it is still a unique antiquing experience. To buy or sell there is not for the faint of heart. You have to know your merchandise and values, because every dealer and collector there will know. They are shrewd and savvy collectors, some of whom have been buying and selling at that market for many years.

My only regret is that I didn't go to the LaChute Market years ago. It is still a fascinating event to attend for anyone seriously or even mildly inter- ested in Canadian antiques and collectables.

Ken Lawless' antique store in Spencerville, ON, 1993.

## 19

# COMING FULL CIRCLE

I went to one of my first country auctions in the village of Finch, Ontario in the autumn of 1981. I remember it vividly because it was actually a second date for Joan and me. Earlier, I had been to a few auctions in the mid to late 1970s around the Kemptville area. My previous girlfriend's parents had restored a stone house there in 1967 and filled it with mostly refinished country furniture, but we had gone separate ways, and in the intervening years I developed interests other than antiques.

On this particular day in Finch, they were auctioning the contents of a small yellow bungalow that was built around 1935. The auctioneer used the side porch as his platform and the helpers brought antique after antique out of the house to display before the expectant crowd. It was a classic autumn day in Eastern Ontario; the leaves were changing, there was a touch of coolness in the air, but the sun was shining and kept everyone reasonably warm.

I knew next to nothing about antiques at that time. Joan and I stood there and watched what, I now realize, were some pretty stunning antiques and accessories come out of that little bungalow. The parade included pieces of decorated stoneware, small wooden storage containers, wall boxes, paintings, quilts, and hooked rugs.

Larger pieces of furniture were arranged around the yard. Not one but *two* glazed, flat-to-the-wall cupboards had been extracted from the garage where they were being used for storage. Both cupboards were covered with dust and grime. Cobwebs hung from their cornices. Some of the panes of glass in the doors were cracked or missing. I remember thinking, "Who could possibly be interested in those two old pieces of junk!" How little I knew.

One particular individual bought a range of items that day. In fact, he seemed to be buying the majority of the good antiques. He was an older man, likely in his late 50s or early 60s, with a silvery beard and sporting a

159

jaunty Fedora. I remember turning to someone on my right, and asking, Who is that man?" "Oh, that's Ken Lawless," a woman replied.

I soon discovered that Ken had a shop in Spencerville and it wasn't long after that sale in Finch that I started to visit him. His antique store was formerly a "carriage" shop – an old, crooked, clapboard building that was plugged full of country furniture and accessories. There was just enough room left for a narrow aisle that led from the front of the store to the back. There were cupboards, harvest tables, chairs, grandfather clocks, paintings, and smaller items everywhere. The second level was full as well. At first, Ken was fairly reserved, but if your interest in antiques, especially country antiques, was genuine, he accepted you unconditionally as a fellow collector, picker, and friend.

I was fascinated by his stories about picking and the great finds he made along the way. Ken was a stickler about "provenance" and most of the furniture in his store had a small strip of masking tape on which he had written the price and the family name of the people who had previously owned the piece.

Over the years, even the rambling old carriage house wasn't sufficient to hold all of Ken's finds so he rented a former meeting hall and stuffed it full of cupboards, chests, and tables. Ken and his wife, Doris, lived on the main street of Spencerville in a large two-storey stucco home. It, too, was filled to the brim with choice antiques and collectibles.

Ken's interests in Canadian antiques encompassed just about every facet of the field, including cast iron stoves, log homes, and buildings. The two stoves he liked best were made by Bélanger and LeGary. And, the models he preferred, as I recall, were the *President* by Bélanger and the LeGary *Rural*.

These kitchen stoves were wood-burning behemoths bristling with sparkling chrome details that contrasted sharply against their coal-black cooking surfaces. The rear wall of the stove below the warming oven was covered with decorative ceramic tiles. On the *President* each tile sported the image of a beaver. Nothing makes a statement quite like the hulking presence of a Bélanger *President* wood stove. And even though one stove must weigh 400 pounds, Ken made a routine habit of buying them at every opportunity. I should add, though, that he made an important distinction between true cast iron cook stoves and ones that came later, the insides of which were made from tin. They may have looked impressive with lots of chrome on the exterior but the "insides" burned out after extensive use. As I recall, the Findlay *Universal* stove fell into this latter category.

A small pine bench from Prescott ON, c. 1850, purchased from Ken Lawless. Possibly a Markey family piece.

In 1984 we were living in Pembroke and by that time, I had started doing some picking of my own. One day I was touring through the countryside on Allumette Island, which is situated in the Ottawa River near Pembroke. I stopped at a small farm and a man came to the back door when I knocked. We chatted briefly and I told him I was there to see if he might have any old hand-made furniture for sale. He asked me into the rear summer kitchen. I took one or two steps in the door, and was staring at the massive form of a Bélanger *President* wood stove standing against the wall facing me. Beside it, on the right hand wall, was an impressive pine pail stand in over paint.

We chatted for a few minutes and I brought up the subject of the wood stove. To my surprise, he said he would sell it – and the pail stand too. We agreed on a price of $600 for the pair. I explained that I had to call a friend to come and help with the stove. He agreed. Later that day, I telephoned Ken and a day or so after we made our way back to the farm on Allumette Island to pick up the stove and the pail stand.

From the moment Ken approached the stove, it was clear that he had had many encounters with them in the past. He quickly detached the vertical stovepipe. Then, at the back of the stove, using a hammer and a chisel, he quickly severed the bolts that held the upper section of the stove to the base. We loaded that piece into the truck then returned and removed the various cast iron lids and the iron frame of the cooking section. That left just the base, which, by now, stripped of several parts, was relatively easy to lift. The two of us managed to carry it across the room and out to the truck.

Ken was happy to buy both the stove and the pail stand from me. That was the only time I ever picked a cast iron stove. It was only one but it was the best one – the Bélanger *President*.

Over the years, I continued to sell antiques to Ken. On several occasions I also purchased antiques from him. Most importantly, though, I learned important lessons from Ken. It was he who told me that if an antique is missing a section or a part to always ask about it and search adjacent buildings and rooms to see if you can find the missing portion.

One day I was picking near Pembroke and stopped at an early Germanic farm. In one of the out buildings, the farmer showed me a pine food locker in original red paint. But there was a problem with it: someone had cut about 12 inches off the base of the cupboard.

"Well, it was a good cupboard at one point in time. But someone's cut it," I said to the farmer.

"I can see that," he said. "But it wasn't me."

"Do you the think the missing bottom part might still be around?"

"Maybe. I don't know."

"Would you mind if we took a look around and see if we can find it."

"No, I don't mind," he replied.

We began the search in the building we were in but had no success. We moved on the building next to it and to another and finally came to a small tool shed. He pulled open the door and walked in. It took a moment for my eyes to adjust to the reduced visibility in the building. There was nothing resembling the cupboard bottom on the floor or on the workbench. I scanned the walls above. I stopped. There above the work bench, nailed securely to the wall and being used as a holder for long handled tools, was the bottom section of the red locker.

"There it is!" I exclaimed.

"Do you think so?' the farmer asked.

"For sure! I know that's it!

"I guess you're right," he replied.

"Do you think you could do without it? I'd like to restore the cupboard and put that base back on it."

"If you're going to restore it, then you can have the base," he said.

"Excellent," I said.

It took several minutes but I was able to remove the base from the wall and put it in the back of my truck with the rest of the cupboard. I gave the farmer $100, took the locker home, and put it in the garage. I propped the upper section on the base to see what it would have looked like originally. It was in rough shape but I was certain that it could be restored. The locker remained in the garage for a few weeks until Ken came by one day. He looked at the piece and asked if he could buy it. I agreed. The food locker went into the back of his truck along with a few other antiques he had come to see.

A few months later, I visited Ken at his new home near Spencerville. I say *new* but actually it is a period log home that Ken had carefully constructed from two vintage buildings that he had disassembled and moved to the site several years earlier. Every square foot of the property and the log home displayed Ken's love and fascination with Canadian country antiques and accessories. He constructed the log home exactly as it would have been back in the day, including "blueing" the interior walls of the sitting room with a historically accurate plaster treatment. Of course the interior was furnished with country furniture and accessories including two large tile-back, cast-iron wood stoves.

Driving up to the building I noticed the food locker on his porch. The base had been securely reattached to the case and while considerably shorter than the original, it was again serving a useful purpose and ready for another 100 years of existence. I like to think that, between us, we had rescued a piece of Canadian Germanic material history.

One Saturday afternoon I met Ken in Spencerville when he had just returned from an auction in Perth. In the back of his truck there was an impressive pine sideboard in original colour. Ken said he had purchased it earlier that day at an auction. I took another look at the sideboard, asked for a price, and bought it on the spot. It went from the back of his truck into mine. I still own it to this day.

On another Saturday in the autumn of 1983, Joan and I went to an auction near Ferguson's Falls in Lanark County. The only item of interest was a small stretcher-based tavern table and I was determined to buy it. An hour or so later, Ken showed up and I knew he would instantly spot the table. A few minutes later we met and decided to flip a coin for the table. I won the toss and he left for another auction. The auctioneer soon put up the table and I was the successful bidder. A year or so afterwards, when we were preparing for the move to Pembroke, I sold several antiques to Ken, including that little Lanark County tavern table. So, in the end, he got it anyway!

On a hot July summer day, Joan and I attended a farm auction on County Road 6, just south of the town of Renfrew. After arriving at the sale, my attention was immediately drawn to a small pine open dish-dresser that was propped up against the house near the front porch. It was quite primitive but the construction was not without integrity and the maker had tried to embellish the cupboard by adding a saw tooth cornice and a decorative cut-out along the base. Most impressive was that the cupboard was in original dark-red paint. While there was some competition for it, the auctioneer knocked it down to me for $350. Joan and I loaded it into the back of my 1983 GMC S15 half-ton and drove over to our friend's cottage on the Ottawa River, where we enjoyed the rest of the day by the water. The little open dish-dresser spent the next several months in the living room of our apartment in Ottawa. In preparation for the move to Pembroke that autumn, we made the decision to sell it. It went with Ken into the load with the Lanark County tavern table.

What I valued most about my relationship with Ken Lawless was the stories we used to exchange about "great finds." Of course, he had many more to relate than I did. But over the intervening 25 years or so, I had acquired my share too. It was always a treat to sit down with Ken and trade anecdotes about antiques we had found. Ken has a terrific memory and, during a story, takes great pains to recall the specific concession road and the name of the family from which he bought a particular antique.

When I last saw him, Ken mentioned that he was "in his 83rd year." We sat in his new home in Prescott, Ontario with his charming wife, Doris, by his side, and talked for an hour. We reminisced about great cupboards, super harvest tables, and wonderful pieces of stoneware and folk art. He was quiet at first but before long, his blue eyes lit up with excitement and a little smile kept crossing his face as we recalled the thrill of the hunt and the satisfaction of acquiring the antiques we chased throughout the years.

Toward the end of our conversation, I told him about the book I was writing and mentioned that I wanted to include a chapter about him. He looked across at me and said quietly, "I would be honoured to be in your book, Shaun."

Before leaving that day, Ken and I wandered outside. The garage door was open and we examined the antiques that he had stored against an interior wall. Included among them was a magnificent stoneware water cooler with the image of a large bird in cobalt blue glaze painted on the front. It was a stunning piece of work and I'm sure Ken noticed my reaction when I saw it sitting there on top of a blanket chest.

"What would something like be worth?"

"$2,500," Ken replied, without missing a beat. And then he told me the exact location of the farm from which he had bought it many years earlier.

After admiring the piece of stoneware for a few moments, Ken and I shook hands and said goodbye. As I walked down the laneway to my car parked at the edge of the street, I realized there was symmetry to the moment. I was at a home in Prescott, with the man I had first seen at that auction in Finch in 1981, admiring a piece of stoneware that was eerily similar to the one Joan and I had unearthed just a few miles away, also in 1981. Those years had come full circle.

Joan Markey in Throoptown in 1981 holding a shard from the Gallagher and McCauley butter churn.

Ken Lawless is only one of the interesting characters I have met through antiques. Few collectors bring it all together the way he has: the land, the restored vintage home, the business and an impressive collection of museum-quality antiques. Of anyone I met in my years of collecting, Ken accomplished that feat probably best of anyone. He personifies what antique collecting is all about: discovery, knowledge, competition, companionship, fascination, respect for the people who settled this country, and for the artifacts of their lives they left behind.

At an auction in the Ottawa Valley, 1984, I'm in the yellow ball cap.

# 20

## Antiques and the Rhythm of Life

H unting successfully for Canadian antiques and folk art has paid dividends in more ways than one. I credit antique collecting for my success in business as an independent consultant.

In the spring of 1996, I was essentially unemployed, having been unceremoniously bumped out of my government job after 10 years of service. It was the first time in my working career that I was out of a job. I was middle-aged, mostly unilingual English (a career-limiting status in government-dominated Ottawa) and, at 48, my employment prospects were not encouraging. I was bitter, angry, and more than a little scared about my future prospects. What's more, the country was still in recovery from the recession that had begun in 1991. I knew in my gut that "consulting" was most likely the only avenue open to me professionally. Although I knew something about "communications" and was a reasonably good writer, I had never had a consulting contract in my life.

Regardless of motivation, for most occupations in life one must be willing and able to meet a defined standard. The standards are readily visible for most occupations: law, medicine, accounting, financial services, engineering, etc. The qualifications necessary to be a consultant are far less visible. The qualifications necessary to be an antique picker and collector are non-existent. You make those up on your own – by doing it.

So, while I may have had zero experience in consulting, by 1996 I had been collecting and dealing in antiques for 15 years. And, while I could possibly have made antiques my profession at that point, I thought a career in some form of communications consulting was still possible and likely more profitable.

In those early days, despite the fact that Ottawa was brimming with consultants of all stripes, I kept telling myself that there had to be room for one more. I would continue antique collecting and dealing in the background, but my plan was to concentrate on building a communications consulting practice. I knew the hunt for consulting contracts would be frustrating, difficult, and at times depressing. I hoped that the hunt for antiques would continue to provide some measure of success in a different field and help keep me sane while I sought out consulting contracts.

I don't particularly like networking and cold-calling. In my case, there was added discomfort because I was out of work and presenting myself as a consultant with no experience. Being unemployed, especially newly unemployed, brings with it certain psychological baggage. It's embarrassing and humbling. The fog of unemployment surrounds you, sapping your enthusiasm and draining your energy.

Each week, I forced myself to make cold calls and attend events where I could network, meet people, and possibly find consulting contracts. The summer of 1996 came and went. On days when I couldn't face the consulting hunt, I opted instead to hunt for antiques. Driving in the Ottawa Valley on a beautiful summer day, meeting friendly people, finding and buying antiques stood in stark contrast to the increasingly frustrating and uncomfortable experience of looking for consulting work.

In the autumn of 1996, I noticed an advertisement for a career fair at a local technology company. I showed the advertisement to Joan.

"Why don't you go," she said. "It would be interesting."

I was not enthusiastic. I knew there would be hundreds of people in attendance and my skill set was not in demand by technology companies. I said as much to Joan. She tossed my argument aside. "Oh, why not do it. Go for an hour."

Against my nature, I grudgingly agreed to attend the event and later that week found myself at a company's headquarters in suburban Ottawa. As I suspected, there were hundreds of people in the line. I couldn't help noticing that I was the only one with grey hair! I could feel my mood going from bad to worse.

To their credit, the company's event was well managed. I had a friendly interview with a human resources officer. There was even an opening in their marketing communications area, which was relevant to my experience. They kept my resume and I returned home feeling satisfied that I had at least attended the event.

The next day, I decided to write about my experience at the career fair.

My articles from *The Globe and Mail*.

In a couple of hours, I wrote a story about it, printed a copy, and threw it in a drawer.

A couple of weeks later, I heard through a contact that an editor at *The Globe and Mail* newspaper was looking for "stringers," or freelance writers. I decided to make a cold call to Gordon Pitts, a senior editor with the newspaper. Gord was editing the Globe's *Managing Page* feature. Previously, he had worked for the *Ottawa Citizen*. I remember our exchange on the telephone vividly. After a brief introduction, I blurted. "I heard that you were looking for freelance writers."

"Actually, I'm not," was his reply. An uncomfortable silence followed.

"Oh, well I must have my information wrong then. Sorry to have bothered you," I said.

"No problem," Gord replied.

I was just about to hang up when I heard him say. "Well, do you have any samples of your work you could send me?"

I could hear the noise of the newsroom clearly in the background.

"Ah, sure. Sure, I can send you some things I've written."

"Do it. I'll have a look at them."

"I will. I'll send them right away. And, thanks."

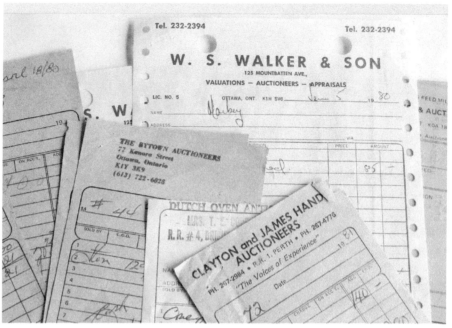

Auction receipts for antiques I've purchased.

The next morning I began searching through my files for samples of written work to send to Gord. I managed to find a few items written while working in my last job. They were far from inspiring but it was all I had. They made for a small and unimpressive pile of writings. Just then, rummaging through files and drawers, I came across the piece I wrote about attending the career fair. I held it in my hand. Should I include it in the package? Maybe I shouldn't. After all, it practically screamed "unemployed"! I didn't want to present myself as unemployed. I waffled. I put it in the envelope. I took it out. Finally, against my better judgment, I stuffed it in the envelope and sealed it. Later that morning, I posted the envelope to Gord.

A week or so later, I was sitting at a desk in the offices of a friend of mine who had graciously invited me to use his facilities during my job search. I had free use of the office equipment, telephones, and meeting space. The phone on my desk rang and I picked it up.

"This is Gord Pitts from the Globe," said the voice on the other end of the line.

"Gord! Hi." I replied, taken aback to hear from him.

"Shaun, I got that package with the samples of your writing."

"Oh good. That's good." I stammered nervously.

"That piece about the career fair?"

"Yes?"

"I'd like to publish that piece."

I was stunned. *The Globe and Mail*, Canada's largest newspaper wanted to publish something I had written!

"Sure! That would be great! Go ahead." I quickly replied.

"I'm going to run it as a guest-type column. Should be out in a week or so."

We agreed to a modest figure for the rights to publish the article and then he hung up. I stared down at the desk in front of me. I felt my throat tighten, my eyes got watery. It was an emotional moment; one that I will always remember.

*The Globe and Mail* published my column and it was one of my proudest professional moments when I picked up the paper that day, found the *Managing Page*, and saw the story with my "byline" in small bold type below the headline. It may have been only one article, just 700 words, but this was vindication. This was an endorsement of me as a writer. This was proof that my search for a new professional status had finally produced a solid and tangible result.

I went on to write several more articles and columns for the newspaper. It was a privilege to write for the Globe and to work for Gordon Pitts, who was a demanding but receptive and patient editor throughout that year. It was, at the time, the best professional experience of my career and I will always remember *The Globe and Mail* and Gordon Pitts for making it happen.

The visibility I received as a freelancer led indirectly to my first real consulting work. A new high technology company in Ottawa asked me to handle their media relations.

When more companies asked me to help them with their media relations needs, I had to make a difficult choice between the two occupations. Somewhat reluctantly, I chose media relations. My stint as a columnist and journalist was over. However, my new career as a media relations consultant was accelerating. Ottawa's technology sector was booming, and before long I had a growing stable of corporate clients. *Shaun Markey Communications Inc.* was born and flourished. I had real clients, real consulting work, and an exciting new field in which to work.

Before long, I was enjoying success in both consulting and the antiques field and that success continued unabated for the next five years. And although the recession in 2001 took a toll on my consulting business, by that time I was well established and managed to weather the recession and en-

Haying in the 1920s by F. Bailey, Shawville QC, 1990.

joyed a return to the same high levels of business for another five years between 2003 and 2008.

Antiques are not immune to recessions. Poor economic times take a toll on antique dealers and antiques in general. But, while a recession may dampen the price of antiques for a time, the industry tends to come roaring back when the economy recovers. Antiques share the same key characteristic as land. Forgeries aside, they are not making any more of them.

I am sure that I would not have come close to the success I had in consulting if it hadn't been for the knowledge and experience gained from antique collecting – and specifically, the *process* of antique collecting.

Searching for antiques, negotiating their purchase, and researching the items is much the same as searching for and winning consulting contracts. Most importantly, being a successful antique collector requires persistence, patience, strategy, and creative thinking. Again, these characteristics are also required of a successful consultant.

Antique collecting has also taught me to be more observant and has sharpened my eye for details. Dealing in antiques has helped me become a better negotiator and better in business generally.

It is easy to find antiques if they are in plentiful supply. It is relatively easy to find consulting contracts in a buoyant and bullish economy. It's an entirely different matter when one must find antiques when they are scarce;

when one desires a certain antique; when that particular type of item is rare. Desire drove me to a level of success in antiques. *Need* drove me to the level of success I've had in my consulting business.

As I write these words, we are still suffering the effects of the economic crisis of 2008. This time, the recession, at least from my perspective, has been longer and deeper than others I have experienced.

My consulting business is lagging and I hear from talking to other dealers and collectors that antiques are sluggish too. The future in business is at best unclear.

Searching for antiques and folk art has taught me to never give up. In business, it has taught me to think creatively and to push myself beyond my limits. Through antiques, I have discovered strengths and abilities I didn't know I possessed. Antiques and folk art have enriched my life immeasurably.

I may never again enjoy the success in business or antique hunting that I had in earlier years, and if that's the case, I'll accept the fact. However, I do know one thing with certainty. I'll keep on searching, knowing that the next important discovery or accomplishment in life may be just around the next bend in the road.

With a Joe Norris cove scene painted in 1981.

# EPILOGUE

I have an old photograph album that holds many images of the antiques we have found and the auctions we have attended over the years. Each page is a stiff piece of cardboard with a transparent piece of plastic over it. You peel back the plastic sheet and arrange your photos behind it. I referred to it often while I was writing, and several of the photographs are reproduced in this book.

I can't help but notice in the older photos that, back then, my stomach was flat and I had dark hair on top of my head where there is none today. I realize, too, that I have significantly more of a "collecting" past than I do a future.

Since my first purchase, over 30 years has passed like a flash. I guess time does that when you enjoy what you're doing. I continue to search for Canadian antiques and folk art. To this day, my blood still runs faster every time I am on the trail of another potential find. I still enjoy getting out on the back roads of Eastern Ontario and Western Quebec, looking for antiques and folk art. The adrenaline still flows when I see an interesting and important antique or piece of folk art.

The urge to collect has always been with me. As a child, I collected comics, IGA gold bond stamps, bubble gum cards, and even the tiny comic papers in which each piece of gum was wrapped. Apparently, collecting is embedded deeply within my DNA.

When I had finished writing about half of this book, I printed off the pages and put them in a three-ring binder to take to someone whose opinion of the book would mean more to me than anyone else: my mother, Rita M. Markey.

We sat together in her room at her retirement residence and I put the blue binder into her hands. Now in her 92nd year, my Mum is still a voracious reader and she happily and easily ploughs through two or three books a week. As a former member of the Hansard Staff on Parliament Hill who transcribed thousands of pages of parliamentary debates and reached a typing speed of 108 words per minute on a manual typewriter, she is a stickler for correct grammar and accurate punctuation. While she will never be my harshest critic, I knew having her read this book would be an important Litmus test of the quality of my literary effort.

She was excited and pleased to know that I had been writing a book about my adventures in antiques. She opened the binder and began reading while I sat opposite her on the couch. After a few minutes I stood and took a few steps forward until I could see through the patio window of her apartment. Light was fading on that beautiful evening in May.

Fittingly, the building in which she lives is situated beside a century-old, gracious Georgian stone home that fronts on the historic Richmond Road, one of the oldest thoroughfares in the Ottawa area and one of the first settlement roads that was built linking Bytown, as Ottawa was known then, to the settlements in the Ottawa Valley. Between the stately stone home and my mother's building is an enchanting walled garden which, on that night, was nicely in bloom and members of the public were wandering through its paths, enjoying the new flowers.

To the right, I could see the Ottawa River, swollen from the spring run-off, flowing silently, majestically, from its origins far beyond the western horizon; this is the vital waterway that so many Ontario and Quebec early settlers used in the 19th century to journey to their new homes and to live along its welcoming but challenging shores, filled with the hopes and dreams that only a new country could offer them. I enjoyed the view for a few moments then returned to my seat.

As she continued to read and turned the pages, a little smile appeared on her face and she slowly began nodding her head, I hoped, in approval. I interrupted her reading.

"Well, what do think Mum?"

My mother paused from the pages in front of her, the smile still playing across her face. She looked across at me.

"Oh Shaunie," she said. "It's good. Very good. I really like it."

I was happy to share this unique moment with my mother and pleased that she enjoyed what I had written.

It is my sincere hope that anyone who picks up this book and decides to invest the time to read it will enjoy it, too. Perhaps a comment I made in the Introduction is worth repeating: the timing is perfect for anyone who wishes to start collecting Canadian antiques.

My mother and I sit at the edge of the walled garden beside the Maplelawn stone house, Ottawa ON, 2012.

Despite the fact that television has recently glamourized antiques and picking, today's younger generations do not seem compelled to collect Canada's past. The antique industry in Canada is largely unorganized and, while the professional associations do what they can to promote Canada's material history, more should be done by everyone involved, including government at all levels.

What is it about antiques that piqued my interest so intensely over 30 years ago and which continues to hold me in its grasp? For me, it started when I wanted to know about my family, my ancestors, those who had gone before me in this world. Who were they? How and where did they live? What were the things that they constructed and used? Finding the answers to those questions led, by extension, to an interest in the objects and decorations that other people had created with such care and devotion and used throughout their lives. Through their creations, we can catch a glimpse of their lives – how they stored their precious possessions, the cupboards they used to display their finer things. People who first came to this country and settled it tried to bring a sense of improvement and a finer quality of life that is reflected in the items they used everyday and for special purposes.

When you pick up an antique made in an Ontario village or on a farm 150 years ago, you are holding one small piece of an individual's history in your hands – a piece of Canadian history. It's precious.

In a free-market economy we set a value on items, and antiques are no different. We capitalize on fascination with the past, with the objects and possessions of those who went before us. Some people look forward and have a fascination with technology and the future. Some of us look backward and are equally fascinated with the cultural artifacts of our ancestors. It is ironic that innovations in technology, especially the Internet, have advanced the field of antiques, both in terms of the research and the marketing of them.

As I look back on my 32 years of collecting and picking, it occurs to me that there never was going to be a huge Markey Collection. If I had kept everything I found, there certainly would have been a more impressive collection than the one I have now but that's not the way things turned out. I had a foot in both camps. I sold antiques and I collected antiques. I enjoyed both the thrill of finding important antiques and the thrill of selling them, most often, for much more than I paid.

Despite what you may hear, there are still interesting Canadian antiques to be found and enjoyed. When you embrace Canadian antiques you preserve a small piece of our country's past and watch over it until the next generation of collectors takes over from you. Go ahead and discover the world of Canadian antiques. Start collecting. You will not be disappointed. I believe there is something of the collector in all of us. And, who knows, you may be the next great Canadian antique picker!

# Acknowledgements

In my "man cave", Ottawa ON, 2014.

Many individuals have been instrumental in my life as a collector, dealer, and picker of Canadian antiques and folk art.

Joan Markey, my wife, has been a constant companion and supporter of all my efforts in life, most notably antiques and my communications consulting practice.

My parents, Rita M. Markey and the late Edward J. Markey, encouraged me from the outset and were a patient and attentive audience when I talked, on many occasions for far too long, about the antiques and collectibles I found and the corresponding adventures associated with their acquisition.

My sister, Sharon Colle, and her husband, Mike Colle MPP, my brothers Stephen Markey, Scott Markey, Sloan Markey, and the late Stuart Markey, have over the years, either participated in my hunt for Canadian antiques and folk art, helped me at antique shows, or been customers for the objects I found.

Janet Cathcart provided timely and essential advice and counsel to me, not only for this book, but also throughout my career, most importantly in the last 15 years when I was an independent media relations consultant.

Brian and Susan Cathcart read early chapters of this book and challenged me to put more of "myself" it. I hope I've managed to do that.

My good friend, Robin Ritchie, encouraged me throughout the writing of the manuscript, insisted I find an engaging title, and praised the creation of the book by reminding me that many people say they should write a book, whereas very few actually do it.

To the Lindsays: Kate, Courtney and Samantha for their enthusiastic support from the outset. I know Ken would have got a big kick out of the book.

I want to acknowledge Richard Huxtable, with whom I have had an ongoing, friendly, and spirited discussion about antiques for over 30 years.

Ken Lawless of Spencerville taught me important lessons about searching for and finding antiques and folk art.

Gavin Wilson has always been willing to share his insights about picking and finding antiques.

Catharine Somerville was with me when we attended my first country auctions and introduced me to her family's beautifully restored *Stone House* in Kemptville, Ontario and their collection of antiques.

Jason Miskelly, friend, fellow dealer, collector, and picker was a steady customer for many of the antiques and collectibles that I found.

When other dealers couldn't or wouldn't, Clay Benson, on several occasions, stepped up and bought important antiques and folk art from me.

Leonard Lee provided help and assistance and met with me on more than one occasion to offer his advice on printing and publishing. Guy Thatcher also gave me advice on these topics

More recently, my friend, Dr. Martin Osler, persuaded me to again exhibit and sell antiques at the *Bowmanville Antique and Folk Art Show*. I appreciated his friendly and persistent encouragement to do so.

A sincere thank you to Adrian Tinline, creator of the Facebook group, *Canadiana Antiques*, where the first chapters of this book began as postings.

Maria Ford of Kaszas Marketing edited my manuscript, and her thoughtful and insightful suggestions helped strengthen the final product immeasurably.

Todd Coopee of Sonderho Press led me through the printing and publishing process and saved me from any number of mistakes and pitfalls. Denis Savoie's superb book design captured the look and feel I had in mind from the outset. Their professional expertise, not to mention patience and understanding, brought this book to life.

Finally, I want to acknowledge and thank all those individuals who welcomed me into their homes and farmhouses and allowed me to view, and often to purchase, their antiques and collectibles. Without them, there would be no collection and absolutely no book.

# Photo Credits

The professional photographs throughout this book are the excellent work of Matt Zambonin of Ottawa. For more information, visit www.mattzamboninphoto.com

Many of the photographs in this book were quick snaps taken at the time with inexpensive cameras. Thanks to digital technology, we were able to reproduce them and somewhat improve the quality.

I am grateful to Gerry Chartrand (www.gerryspsortscards.com) for providing me with the photos of the C55 hockey cards used in Chapter 3.

Denis Savoie of Sonderho Press provided the barn photo for use in Chapter 6.

The City of Ottawa Archives provided the early photograph of the Rideau Canal with the Bank Street Bridge in the background in Chapter 7 and the photo of the Aberdeen Pavilion building also in Chapter 7.

I want to express my appreciation to Mel Birnkrant for providing me with the photo of the Toonerville Trolley in Chapter 8.

Stephen Harris coordinated the photograph in Chapter 14 of the etched glass advertising panels. The owner, Steven Doherty, graciously allowed me to reproduce the photographs.

John Rawn agreed to photograph his great "folk art" chest of drawers as reproduced in Chapter 16.

Dr. Martin Osler was the eventual and fortunate owner of the little hanging cupboard shown in Chapter 16. He was kind enough to provide me with a photograph for the book.

Ken Lawless sent me photographs from his private albums to reproduce in the Chapter 19.

# FOLK ART IN THE ATTIC ONLINE

If you wish to read more about my life-long hunt for antiques and folk art, subscribe to my blog: www.folkartintheattic.com. And, check out my stories and pictures about Canadian antiques and folk art at these sites:

 http://facebook.com/shaunmarkeyantiques

 http://twitter.com/folkartintheattic

 http://www.pinterest.com/shaunmar/
shaun-markey-antiques-and-folk-art/

CPSIA information can be obtained at www.ICGtesting.com
Printed in the USA
LVOW05s2031280415

436423LV00018B/47/P